Many talk about the value
not showy, seemingly not [
Light helps. Case's thoroug
on—they give shape to you
—PAUL MILLER
Author of *A Pra*...

Children learn to speak by repeating the words they hear from their parents. Similarly, we learn to pray by speaking God's words back to him. In the spirit of Matthew Henry's *Method for Prayer*, Andrew Case helps God's children by putting the Scriptures on their lips as prayers to our Father.
—DR. JOEL R. BEEKE
Author of *Taking Hold of God: Reformed and Puritan Perspectives on Prayer*
President, Puritan Reformed Theological Seminary
Grand Rapids

**COMMENDATION FOR OTHER PRAYER BOOKS BY ANDREW CASE**

The concept of this book is really quite simple—and very helpful: a weaving together of biblical passages turned into prayers for one's wife... a great idea and a most helpful and welcome book!
—JUSTIN TAYLOR
The Gospel Coalition
Crossway senior vice president and publisher

By combining the two greatest powers on earth—scripture and prayer—Andrew Case not only shows husbands how to pray for our wives, but teaches us how to read scripture: prayerfully. This book is a gold mine.
—MIKE MASON
Bestselling author of *The Mystery of Marriage*

Blessed is the wife whose husband offers prayers on her behalf such as those in this book. Blessed is the man who prays them, for by Case's example he will learn how to pray through a passage of Scripture for anything, not just for matters regarding his wife.
—DONALD S. WHITNEY
Author of *Spiritual Disciplines for the Christian Life*

Of all the things a wife can do for her husband, of all the many ways she can show her support, nothing tops the prayers she offers up before the Throne. And it's the wise wife who, when she prays, recognizes how her marriage—even her own life—is being strengthened and deepened. God sees when women kneel in prayer for their husbands, and *Prayers of an Excellent Wife* provides the reader with all the scriptural principles and language needed to cover a man with powerful intercession—prayers so effective, they'll resonate throughout his life.
—JONI EARECKSON TADA
Joni and Friends International Disability Center

Many believers feel paralyzed when it comes time to pray. Case's prayers for a wife illustrate practically and devotionally how scripture should be the fuel for our prayers. Read, meditate, and pray!
—THOMAS R. SCHREINER
James Buchanan Professor of
New Testament Interpretation
The Southern Baptist Theological Seminary
Author of *The King in His Beauty*

What better words to pray for our husbands than the very words of his Maker? *Prayers of an Excellent Wife* provides a guide for humbly engaging in the joyful duty of intercession, petition and thanksgiving for our husbands. I am delighted to speak these prayers with and on behalf of Matt.
—LAUREN CHANDLER
Wife of Matt Chandler who is preaching pastor at The Village Church, Highland Village, TX

There are lots of 'parenting resources' out there for Moms and Dads, on all kinds of important issues ranging from discipline to talking about sex to family vacations. One of the most important responsibilities of fathers and mothers, however, is to pray for and with their children. This book, drawn mostly right from Holy Scripture, can be a spur to your family to get off the couch and away from the television and on your knees praying for the salvation and welfare of your children.
—RUSSELL D. MOORE
Author of *Adopted for Life*
President, Ethics & Religious Liberty Commission

Andrew Case has provided parents with a powerful tool: the Word of God turned to prayer—specifically for their children. What a blessing it is to read that prayer is a reminder of our littleness and of God's greatness. That nowhere are we more helpless than in prayer. For it means we can begin where we are, as we are, today.

Soaked in scripture, interspersed with great quotes, this book will encourage, inspire, and strengthen anyone who wants to learn to grow in dependence on God, or—in other words—prayer.
—SALLY LLOYD-JONES
Best-selling author of *The Jesus Storybook Bible*

As a father, I continually feel inadequate to the task of praying for the three precious children God has entrusted to me. I understand that I need to pray and I genuinely want to pray. Yet I am so often lost when it comes to knowing how. In *Setting Their Hope in God*, Andrew Case turns to the ultimate prayer book, the Bible, to craft prayers for parents who want to see their children turn to the Lord, to live for the Lord, to honor him with their lives. I am convinced that this book will prove an indispensable resource to many mothers and fathers as they seek to hold up their children before the throne of grace.
—TIM CHALLIES, author, blogger, www.challies.com

for

כי אחתי ותאמי־תאומים

Based on *The Holy Bible, English Standard Version* copyright ©2001 by Crossway Bibles, a publishing ministry of Good News Publishers. Used by permission. All rights reserved.

Andrew Case, *Praying the Light*

© 2015 by Andrew Case

All rights reserved. Any part of this publication may be shared, provided that you do not charge for or alter the content in any way.
For the free PDF and eBook please visit www.HisMagnificence.com.

ISBN 978-1519428516

# Praying *the* Light

*The unfolding of your words gives light;
it imparts understanding to the simple.*
Psalm 119:130

# Contents

*Prayers*     8
*Appendix:*
    *Books Quoted*     233
    *Further Reading on the Subject of Prayer*     234

*Be encouraged, dear Christian reader, with fresh earnestness to give yourself to prayer, if you can only be sure that you ask for things which are for the glory of God.*
~George Mueller

*If attended to with trust and faith, the Bible is the way to actually hear God speaking and also to meet God himself.... Your prayer must be firmly connected to and grounded in your reading of the Word. This wedding of the Bible and prayer anchors your life down in the real God.* ~Tim Keller

*Prayer, at its best, is the noblest, the sublimest, the most magnificent, and stupendous act that any creature of God can perform on earth or in heaven. Prayer is far too princely a life for most men. It is high, and they are low, and they cannot attain it.*
~Alexander Whyte

O Keeper of Your people,

It is better to take refuge in You than to trust in man. It is better to take refuge in You than to trust in princes. Therefore cause me to take refuge in You alone. Be my strength and my song; be my great salvation.

Let me lift up the cup of salvation and call on Your Name. Open to me the gates of righteousness, that I may enter through them and give thanks to You. Raise my eyes to the hills to see from where my help comes. For my help comes from You, who made heaven and earth. Do not let my foot be moved; keep me and do not slumber. Please keep me and neither slumber nor sleep. Keep me from all evil; keep my life. Keep my going out and my coming in from this time forth and forevermore.

O my soul, do you know who keeps you? The LORD is your keeper; the LORD is your shade on your right hand. The sun shall not strike you by day, nor the moon by night.

Lord Jesus, keep me. May I wait eagerly for Your appearing. Hasten the wonderful day of Your return—the wedding supper of the Lamb. Amen (Psalm 118, 116, 121).

---

*American culture is probably the hardest place in the world to learn to pray. We are so busy that when we slow down to pray, we find it uncomfortable. We prize accomplishments, production. But prayer is nothing but talking to God. It feels useless, as if we are wasting time. Every bone in our bodies screams, "Get to work." ~Paul Miller*

Precious Provider,

Your testimonies are wonderful; therefore my soul keeps them. The unfolding of Your word gives light; it imparts understanding to the simple. May I open my mouth and pant, because I long for Your commandments. Turn to me and be gracious to me, as is Your way with those who love Your name.

Keep steady my steps according to Your promise; let no iniquity get dominion over me. Redeem me from man's oppression, that I may keep Your precepts. Make Your face shine upon me, Your servant, and teach me Your statutes. May my eyes shed streams of tears, because people do not keep Your law (Psalm 119).

*A man cannot live unless he takes his breath,
nor can the soul, unless it breathes forth its desires to God.*
~Thomas Watson

O LORD God of heaven,

The great and awesome God who keeps covenant and steadfast love with those who love Him and keep His commandments, let Your ear be attentive and Your eyes open, to hear the prayer of Your servant that I now pray before You. For I have sinned against You; I have acted very corruptly against You by forsaking the path of righteousness and the fear of You; I have not kept Your commandments, Your statutes, or the rules that You commanded Your servant Moses.

Please forgive and restore me when I am unfaithful to Your Word, when I neglect prayer, fail to redeem the time, speak carelessly, walk foolishly, fail to hope in You, seek great things for myself, become anxious about tomorrow. Do not cease exhorting and reforming me when I am beset with the fear of man, the cares of the world, or the love of money. May I never lose confidence that, in spite of my many iniquities and shortcomings, I am Your servant whom You have redeemed by Your great power and by Your strong hand.

O Lord, let Your ear be attentive to the prayer of Your servant, for I delight to fear Your name. Give success to me today, and grant me mercy (Nehemiah 1).

# Merciful Master,

Look on my affliction and deliver me, and let me not forget Your law. Plead my cause and redeem me; give me life according to Your promise! Salvation is far from the wicked, for they do not seek Your statutes. Great is Your mercy, O LORD; give me life according to Your rules. Even when my persecutors and adversaries are many, let me not swerve from Your testimonies. May I look at the faithless with pity, because they do not keep Your commands. Consider how I love Your precepts! Give me life according to Your steadfast love. The sum of Your word is truth, and every one of Your righteous rules endures forever (Psalm 119).

*To begin the day with prayer is but a formality unless it go on in prayer, unless for the rest of it we pray in deed what we began in word. One has said that while prayer is the day's best beginning it must not be like the handsome title-page of a worthless book. ~ P. T. Forsyth*

Sovereign Preserver,

Let me stand up and bless You our God from everlasting to everlasting. Blessed be Your glorious name, which is exalted above all blessing and praise. You are the LORD, You alone. You have made me. You have made heaven, the heaven of heavens, with all their host, the earth and all that is on it, the seas and all that is in them; and You preserve all of them; and the host of heaven worships You.

Thank You for preserving me, for keeping me as Your chosen, for directing my steps on the narrow way. Please continue to preserve my life! For You are the LORD, the God who chose me and brought me out of darkness and made my heart faithful before You. Thank You that You have kept the promises that are mine in Christ Jesus, for You are righteous. I praise You that You are a God ready to forgive, gracious and merciful, slow to anger and abounding in steadfast love, and have not departed from me. Even when I stray and my heart grows dull, You in Your great mercies have not forsaken me. Therefore, keep on making a name for Yourself through me, and instruct me with Your good Spirit. Amen (Nehemiah 9).

Ruler of the world,

    Put Your Spirit in me with perfect power and bear His fruits from my life. May I be a loving person; a joyful, peaceful person; patient, kind, and good. Make my soul and actions abound with faithfulness, gentleness, and self-control, for against such things there is no law. By Christ Jesus crucify my flesh with its passions and desires. Let me not grow weary in doing good, for in due season I will reap if I do not give up. And may I never boast except in the cross of our Lord Jesus Christ, by which the world has been crucified to me, and I to the world (Galatians 5 & 6).

*Prayer seem'd to be natural to me; as the breath, by which the inward burnings of my heart had vent.* ~Jonathan Edwards

Great God,

May I be a person inclined to pour myself out for the hungry and satisfy the desire of the afflicted, so that my light will rise in the darkness and my gloom be as the noonday. Then guide me continually and satisfy my desire in scorched places. Make my bones strong, so that I am like a watered garden, like a spring of water, whose waters do not fail.

May I be radiant; my heart thrilled to say, "I will greatly rejoice in the LORD; my soul shall exult in my God, for He has clothed me with the garments of salvation; He has covered me with the robe of righteousness." Make me count the garments of salvation as sufficient clothing, valued by me as more precious and worthy of care than the finest adornments. May my robes of righteousness be ever prevalent, outshining worldly dress. Amen (Isaiah 58 & 61).

Righteous are You, O LORD, and right are Your rules.

You have appointed Your testimonies in righteousness and in faithfulness. May zeal consume me when my foes forget Your words. Your promise is well tried; may I love it. Even when I am small and despised, let me not forget Your precepts. Your righteousness is righteous forever, and Your law is true. When trouble and anguish find me out, make Your commandments my delight. Your testimonies are righteous forever; give me understanding that I may live.

With my whole heart I cry; answer me, O LORD! Cause me to keep Your statutes. I call to You; save me, that I may observe Your testimonies. I rise before dawn and cry for help; may I hope in Your words. Awaken my eyes before the watches of the night, that I may meditate on Your promise. Hear my voice according to Your steadfast love; O LORD, according to Your justice give me life. When they draw near who persecute me with evil purpose, who are far from Your law, assure me that You are near, O LORD, and all Your commandments are true. Long have I known from Your testimonies that You have founded them forever (Psalm 119).

*What makes a heart upright and what makes prayers pleasing to God is a felt awareness of our tremendous need for mercy.*
~John Piper

My Gracious Master,

Cause me to work out my own salvation with fear and trembling, knowing all the while that it is You who work in me, both to will and to work for Your good pleasure.

May I rejoice in You always, and let my reasonableness be known to everyone. Please let me not be anxious about anything, but in everything by prayer and supplication with thanksgiving may I make known my requests to You. And all this so that Your peace, which surpasses all understanding, may guard my heart and mind in Christ Jesus.

Finally Father, make me think on whatever is true, whatever is honorable, whatever is just, whatever is pure, whatever is lovely, whatever is commendable, on anything of excellence, and anything worthy of praise. Through Your Son and for Your glory I ask these things. Amen (Philippians 2 & 4).

*Couples who do not pray are as badly off as those who stop sleeping together. Like lovemaking, prayer requires, in a sense, taking off the clothes, removing the shoes to touch holy ground.*
~Mike Mason

Heavenly Father,

As for me, my prayer is to You. At an acceptable time, O God, in the abundance of Your steadfast love answer me in Your saving faithfulness. And my prayer is this: deliver me from sinking in the mire of sin; let me be delivered from the deep waters of vanity. Let not the flood sweep over me, or the deep swallow me up, or the pit of despair close its mouth over me. Answer me, O LORD, for Your steadfast love is good; according to Your abundant mercy turn to me. Draw near to my soul, redeem me; ransom me because of my frailty.

When I am afflicted and in pain, let Your salvation, O God, set me on high! Then may I praise Your Name with a song, and magnify You with thanksgiving. May I seek You, and rejoice and be glad in You!

O my soul, because you love His salvation, say evermore, "God is great!" Hasten to me, O God! You are my help and my deliverer; O LORD, do not delay! Save me for Your marvelous Name (Psalm 69 & 70).

Blessed God,

Although princes may persecute me without cause, may I stand in awe of Your words. Might I, by the power of Your Spirit, rejoice at Your word like one who finds great spoil. Make me hate and abhor falsehood, but love Your law. May I be someone who praises You seven times a day for Your righteous rules. Great peace have those who love Your law; nothing can make them stumble. May I hope for Your salvation, O Lord, and do Your commandments. Cause my soul to keep Your testimonies and love them exceedingly. Help me to keep Your precepts and testimonies, for all my ways are before You.

Let my cry come before You, O Lord; give me understanding according to Your word! Let my plea come before You; deliver me according to Your word. May my lips pour forth praise, for You teach me Your statutes. May my tongue sing of Your word, for all Your commandments are right. Let Your hand be ready to help me, for I have chosen Your precepts. Create in me a longing for Your salvation, O Lord, and a delight in Your law. Let my soul live and praise You, and let Your rules help me. When I go astray like a lost sheep, seek me, Your servant, for I do not forget Your commandments. Amen (Psalm 119).

*You often feel that your prayers scarcely reach the ceiling; but, oh, get into this humble spirit by considering how good the Lord is, and how evil you all are, and then prayer will mount on wings of faith to heaven. The sigh, the groan of a broken heart, will soon go through the ceiling up to heaven, aye, into the very bosom of God.* ~Charles Simeon

༺❦༻

*Even skeptical Dan prayed, his skepticism falling away from him like a discarded garment in this valley of the shadow, which sifts out hearts and tries souls, until we all, grown-up or children, realize our weakness, and, finding that our own puny strength is as a reed shaken in the wind, creep back humbly to the God we have vainly dreamed we could do without.*
~L.M. Montgomery

Lord Jesus,

It is by Your undying death and willing sacrifice that I come to my Father who has loved me with an everlasting love for no reason but His own purpose and glory. And so I ask, LORD and Sovereign, that I would be blessed because my way is blameless; that I would walk in the law of the LORD! Cause me to keep Your testimonies and seek You with my whole heart, doing no wrong but walking in Your ways.

May I keep Your precepts diligently for love of Your great Name. Oh, that my ways may be steadfast in keeping Your statutes! May my eyes be fixed unswervingly on all Your commandments. Please ignite such joy in me that I must praise You with an upright heart when I learn Your righteous rules. And cause me to keep Your statutes; do not utterly forsake me!

Keep my way pure by teaching me to guard it according to Your word. Let me seek You with my whole heart; let me not wander from Your commandments. May I store up Your word in my heart that I might not sin against You. Blessed are You, O LORD; teach me Your statutes!

May my lips declare the rules of Your mouth, and cause me to delight in the way of Your testimonies as much as in all riches. Quicken my mind to meditate on Your precepts and fix my eyes on Your ways. May I delight in Your statutes and not forget Your word (Psalm 119).

*How much my father's prayers at this time impressed me I can never explain, nor could any stranger understand. When, on his knees and all of us kneeling around him in Family Worship, he poured out his whole soul with tears for the conversion of the Heathen world to the service of Jesus, and for every personal and domestic need, we all felt as if in the presence of the living Savior, and learned to know and love him as our Divine friend.*
~John G. Paton

*We have an allergic reaction to dependency, but this is the state of the heart most necessary for a praying life. A needy heart is a praying heart. Dependency is the heartbeat of prayer.*
~Paul Miller

Ineffable Lover,

Only by the cross do I bring these prayers to You. Do not let my adorning be merely external, but let my adorning be the hidden person of the heart. Give me unity of mind, sympathy, sisterly love, a tender heart, and humility. The end of all things is at hand; therefore let me be self-controlled and sober-minded for the sake of my prayers. Above all, keep me loving others earnestly, since love covers a multitude of sins.

As I have received a gift, may I use it to serve others, as a good steward of Your varied grace. When I speak, let it be as one who speaks the oracles of God; when I serve, as one who serves by the strength that You supply—in order that in everything You may be glorified through Jesus Christ. To You belong glory and dominion forever and ever. Amen (I Peter 3 & 4).

*It is remarkable that in all of his writings Paul's prayers for his friends contain no appeals for changes in their circumstances.*
~Tim Keller

God of my end,

Deal bountifully with me, Your servant, that I may live and keep Your word. And this I ask with importunate reverence: open my eyes, that I may behold wondrous things out of Your law. For I am a mere sojourner on this earth; hide not Your commandments from me! Consume my soul with longing for Your rules at all times, for You rebuke the insolent, accursed ones, who wander from Your commandments. Take away from me scorn and contempt, for I have kept Your testimonies. Cause me to meditate on Your statutes even when princes sit plotting against me. May it be readily on me lips, "Your testimonies are my delight; they are my counselors."

When my soul clings to the dust please give me life according to Your word! When I tell You of my ways, answer me; teach me Your statutes! Make me understand the way of Your precepts and meditate on Your wondrous works.

When my soul melts away for sorrow—for I *will* be well-acquainted with grief if I am Yours—strengthen me according to Your word! I am ever surrounded by false ways in this age; teach me Your law! I have chosen the way of faithfulness; may I set Your rules ever before me. When I cling to Your testimonies, O LORD, let me not be put to shame! Enlarge my heart so that I may run in the way of Your commandments! (Psalm 119).

*How easily we convince ourselves that we are praying to the Lord when in reality we are locked in our own thoughts. We need to ask: If I'm happy, am I really rejoicing in Him, or am I rejoicing in my own self-satisfaction? If I'm worried or afraid, am I truly and humbly asking Him for help, or is my mind busy trying to work out some plan (however spiritual it may seem) for getting myself out of trouble?* ~Mike Mason

Almighty God,

Please teach me the way of Your statutes; may I keep it to the end, as my reward. Give me understanding that I may keep Your law and observe it with my whole heart. Lead me in the path of Your commandments, because I delight in it—O Father, cause me to delight in Your path!

Incline my heart to Your testimonies, and not to selfish gain! Turn my eyes from looking at worthless things; and give me life in Your ways. Confirm to me Your promise, that I may fear You. Turn away the reproach that I dread, for Your rules are good. Behold, may I long for Your precepts; in Your righteousness give me life!

Let Your steadfast love come to me, O LORD, Your salvation according to Your promise; then shall I have an answer for anyone who taunts me, for I trust in Your word. And take not the word of truth utterly out of my mouth, for my hope is in Your rules. May I keep Your law continually, forever and ever, and may I walk in a wide place, for I have sought Your precepts.

Make me also speak of Your testimonies before kings and be not put to shame, for I find my delight in Your commandments, which I love. May I lift up my hands toward Your commandments, and meditate on Your statutes. Amen, come Lord Jesus (Psalm 119).

Father of Wisdom,

Let me never cease to pray for my own life, asking that I may be filled with the knowledge of Your will in all spiritual wisdom and understanding, so as to walk in a manner worthy of You, bearing fruit in every good work and increasing in the knowledge of You. May I be strengthened with all power, according to Your glorious might, for all endurance and patience with joy, giving thanks to You, who have qualified me to share in the inheritance of the saints in light.

Do you remember, O my soul, that He has delivered you from the domain of darkness and transferred you to the kingdom of His beloved Son, in whom you have redemption, the forgiveness of sin? Yes, praise Him for His marvelous grace!

O LORD God, make me continue in the faith, stable and steadfast, not shifting from the hope of the gospel that I heard, which has been proclaimed in all creation under heaven. Keep me! Keep me in the love of Christ. Amen (Colossians 1).

*Anyone who would have power in prayer must be merciless in dealing with his own sins.* ~R.A. Torrey

Giver of all,

Remember Your word to Your servant, in which You have made me hope. May my comfort in my affliction be this: that Your promise gives me life. The insolent might utterly deride me, but do not let me turn away from Your law. When I think of Your rules from of old, let me take comfort, O LORD. O that hot indignation might seize me because of the wicked, who forsake Your law. And I ask that Your statutes would be my songs in the house of my sojourning. Cause me to remember Your Name in the night, O LORD, and keep Your law. This blessing has fallen to me, that I have kept Your precepts.

You are my portion; I promise to keep Your words. I entreat Your favor with all my heart; be gracious to me according to Your promise. When I think on my ways, let me turn my feet to Your testimonies; may I hasten and not delay to keep Your commandments. Though the cords of the wicked ensnare me, allow me not to forget Your law. Make me someone who at midnight rises to praise You because of Your righteous rules. Make me the companion of all who fear You, of those who keep Your precepts. The earth, O LORD, is full of Your steadfast love; teach me Your statutes! (Psalm 119).

*Our prayers are heard, not because we are in earnest, not because we suffer, but because Jesus suffered.*
~Oswald Chambers

O God,

Blessed is the person who fears You, who greatly delights in Your commandments! Please continue to mold me into such a person.

Make light dawn in the darkness for me; You are gracious, merciful, and righteous. Grant that I deal generously and lend, conducting my affairs with justice. Let me never be moved; remember me forever.

May I be not afraid of bad news, but make my heart firm, trusting in You. Give me a steady heart, so that from the rising of the sun to its setting I will praise Your glorious Name.

O my soul, trust in the LORD! He is your help and your shield. O my soul, trust in the LORD! He is your help and your shield. You who fear the LORD, trust in Him! He is your help and your shield. For You, O LORD, made heaven and earth! I will bless You, O God, from this time forth and forevermore. Praise the LORD! (Psalm 112, 113, 115).

※

*We are not so foolish as to think we can learn a trade without the diligent use of helps. Shall we think that we may become spiritually skilful and wise in the understanding of this mystery without making any real effort to use the helps God has given us? The most important of them is fervent prayer. Pray with Paul that 'the eyes of your understanding may be enlightened to behold' the glory of God in Christ. Pray that the 'God of our Lord Jesus Christ, the Father of glory, may give to you the spirit of wisdom and revelation in the knowledge of him.' Fill your minds with spiritual thoughts of Christ. Lazy souls do not get the tiniest sight of this glory. The 'lion in the way' deters them from making the slightest effort.* ~John Owen

O Great Upholder of all things,

Please deal with me, Your servant, according to Your word. Teach me good judgment and knowledge, for I believe Your commandments. Let me not go astray before my affliction; assist me now to keep Your word. You are good and do good; teach me Your statutes. Although the insolent may smear me with lies, help me to keep Your precepts with my whole heart. Even though their heart is unfeeling, let me delight in Your law.

Assure me that it is good for me to be afflicted, that I might learn Your statutes. May the law of Your mouth be better to me than thousands of gold and silver pieces. Be exalted, for Your hands have made and fashioned me; give me understanding that I may learn Your commandments. May those who fear You see me and rejoice, because I have hoped in Your word. Remind me, O LORD, that Your rules are righteous, and that in faithfulness You afflict me. Let Your steadfast love comfort me according to Your promise to Your servant.

Let Your mercy come to me, that I may live; for Your law is my delight. Let the insolent be put to shame, because they have wronged me with falsehood; as for me, may I meditate on Your precepts. Let those who fear You turn to me, that they may know Your testimonies. May my heart be blameless in Your statutes, that I may not be put to shame! (Psalm 119).

O timeless Light of lights, Eternal Father,

Make my soul long for Your salvation; may I hope in Your word. My eyes long for Your promise. When will You comfort me? Let me seek the deepest of comfort in Your steadfast love and faithfulness. When I become like a wineskin in the smoke, let me not forget Your statutes. How long must Your servant endure? When will You judge those who persecute me? The insolent have dug pitfalls for me; they do not live according to Your law. All Your commandments are sure; they persecute me with falsehood; help me! When they have almost made an end of me on earth, let me not forsake Your precepts. In Your steadfast love give me life, that I may keep the testimonies of Your mouth.

Forever, O LORD, Your word is firmly fixed in the heavens. Your faithfulness endures to all generations; You have established the earth and it stands fast. By Your appointment they stand this day, for all things are Your servants. If Your law is not my delight, I will surely perish in my affliction. Oh, that I would never forget Your precepts, for by them You have given me life. I am Yours, save me, for I have sought Your precepts. When the wicked lie in wait to destroy me, may I consider Your testimonies. I have seen a limit to all perfection, but Your commandment is exceedingly broad. Give me life in Your ways. Amen. Come, Lord Jesus (Psalm 119).

*It is very apparent from the word of God, that he is wont often to try the faith and patience of his people, when crying to him for some great and important mercy, by withholding the mercy sought, for a season; and not only so, but at first to cause an increase of dark appearances. And yet he, without fail, at last succeeds those who continue instant in prayer, with all perseverance, and will not let him go except he blesses.*
~Jonathan Edwards

༄༅ ༅༄

*In the broader culture and in our churches, we prize intellect, competency, and wealth. Because we can do life without God, praying seems nice but unnecessary. Money can do what prayer does, and it is quicker and less time-consuming. Our trust in ourselves and in our talents makes us structurally independent of God. As a result, exhortations to pray don't stick.*
~Paul Miller

Changeless God,

May I never forget all Your benefits. Help me to remind myself relentlessly of the One who forgives all my iniquity, who heals all my diseases, who redeems my life from the pit, who crowns me with steadfast love and mercy, who satisfies me with good so that my youth is renewed like the eagle's.

Please work righteousness and justice for me when I am oppressed. Make known Your ways and your acts to me.

O my soul, hear again of your marvelous God! The LORD is merciful and gracious, slow to anger and abounding in steadfast love. He will not always chide, nor will He keep His anger forever. He does not deal with you according to your sins, nor repay you according to your iniquities. For as high as the heavens are above the earth, so great is His steadfast love toward those who fear Him; as far as the east is from the west, so far does He remove your transgressions from you.

O LORD, as a father shows compassion to his children, please show compassion to me. For You know my frame; You remember that I am dust (Psalm 103).

*There is nothing in which we need to take so many lessons as in prayer. There is nothing of which we are so utterly ignorant when we first begin; there is nothing in which we are so helpless. ~Alexander Whyte*

Sovereign Creator and Sustainer,

Oh how I love Your law! May it be my meditation all the day. Your commandment makes me wiser than my enemies, for it is ever with me. Grant me more understanding than all my teachers by making Your testimonies my meditation. May I understand more than the aged, because I keep Your precepts. Assist me to hold back my feet from every evil way, in order to keep Your word. May I not turn aside from Your rules, for You have taught me. How sweet are Your words to my taste, sweeter than honey to my mouth! Through Your precepts make me get understanding, and so hate every false way.

Your word is a lamp to my feet and a light to my path. May I swear an oath and confirm it, to keep Your righteous rules. When I am severely afflicted please give me life, O LORD, according to Your word! Accept my free offerings of praise, O LORD, and teach me Your rules. Though I may hold my life in my hand continually, let me not forget Your law. When the wicked lay a snare for me, may I not stray from Your precepts. Make Your testimonies my heritage forever, and the joy of my heart. Incline my heart to perform Your statutes forever, to the end. Amen (Psalm 119).

*How often do little children ask? Repeatedly. Over and over again. They wear us out.* ~Paul Miller

Sweet Sustainer and Rock of Salvation,

I do not ask that You take me out of the world, but that You keep me from the evil one. Sanctify me in the truth; Your word is truth. Father, I desire that I also, whom You have given to Christ, may be with Him where He is, to see His glory that You have given Him because You loved Him before the foundation of the world.

I give thanks to You always because of Your grace that has been given me in Christ Jesus, and I ask that in every way I may be enriched in You in all speech and all knowledge—even that the testimony about Christ might be confirmed in me—so that I will not be lacking in any spiritual gift, as I wait for the revealing of our Lord Jesus Christ, who will sustain me to the end, guiltless in the day of Christ.

O God, be the source of my life in Christ Jesus, whom You made my wisdom and my righteousness and sanctification and redemption. Therefore, let me boast solely in You. For the display of Your wonderful wins-omeness, Amen (John 17 & I Corinthians 1).

*Desire gives fervor to prayer. The soul cannot be listless when some great desire fixes and inflames it...Strong desires make strong prayers...The neglect of prayer is the fearful token of dead spiritual desires...There can be no true praying without desire.* ~E. M. Bounds

O Father of my dearest Lord Jesus,

May I hate the double-minded, but love Your law. Be my hiding place, and my shield; make me hope in Your word. Cause evildoers to depart from me, that I may keep the commandments of my God. Uphold me according to Your promise, that I may live, and let me not be put to shame in my hope! Hold me up, that I may be safe and have regard for Your statutes continually! You spurn all who go astray from Your statutes, for their cunning is in vain. All the wicked of the earth You discard like dross, therefore may I love Your testimonies. My flesh trembles for fear of You, and I am afraid of Your judgments.

I have done what is just and right; do not leave me to my oppressors. Give me a pledge of good; let not the insolent oppress me. May my eyes long for Your salvation and for the fulfillment of Your righteous promise. Deal with me, Your servant, according to Your steadfast love, and teach me Your statutes. I am Your servant; give me understanding, that I may know Your testimonies! It is time for You to act, for Your law has been broken. Therefore, may I cry in my heart, "I love Your commandments above gold, above fine gold. Therefore I consider all Your precepts to be right; I hate every false way." Amen, come Lord Jesus (Psalm 119).

*The Puritans spoke of prayer as oiling the wheels of the soul.*
~J.I. Packer

Our Father in heaven,

Hallowed be Your Name. Please keep Your Name holy in my life. Cause me to consider it reverently in my mind and heart, treating it as sacred by my words and conduct.

May Your kingdom come, and may I long for the day of Your fullness far more than anything else in this life. Stir my heart to seek first Your kingdom.

Your will be done on earth as it is in heaven. Perform Your good pleasure in me—use me as a vessel to magnify the beauty of Your Son. Give me this day my daily bread, providing for my physical needs, for You are a loving, merciful Father who gives good gifts to His children. Teach me to trust You, being not anxious about whether I will have enough for tomorrow.

Forgive me my debts, as I also forgives my debtors. Forgive me when I fall short of Your glory. And form in me a pardoning heart, forbearing in everything.

Lead me not into temptation, but deliver me from evil. Rescue me from the deceitfulness of sin. By Your undeserved mercy keep my heart from being darkened and led into foolishness. For Yours is the kingdom, the power, and the glory forever! Amen (Matthew 6).

*Giving God good advice, and abusing the devil isn't praying.*
~L.M. Montgomery

My Exceeding Joy,

Help me never cease to give thanks to You. May You, the God of my Lord Jesus Christ, the Father of glory, give me a spirit of wisdom and of revelation in the knowledge of You, having the eyes of my heart enlightened, that I may know what is the hope to which You have called me, what are the riches of Your glorious inheritance in the saints, and what is the immeasurable greatness of Your power toward us who believe, according to the working of Your great might.

O Lord, I cannot know and delight in the mystery and beauty of Your gospel unless Your Spirit intervenes, bringing about fruit in me for righteousness. For this reason I bow my knees before You, Father, from whom every family in heaven and on earth is named, that according to the riches of Your glory You may strengthen me with power through Your Spirit in my inner being, so that Christ may dwell in my heart through faith—that I, being rooted and grounded in love, may have strength to comprehend with all the saints what is the breadth and length and height and depth, and to *know* the love of Christ that surpasses knowledge, that I may be filled with all of Your fullness.

Now to You who are able to do far more abundantly than all that I ask or think, according to the power at work within me, to You be glory in the church and in Christ Jesus throughout all generations, forever and ever Amen (Ephesians 1 & 3).

Merciful LORD,

I know that it is Your good pleasure to give of Yourself to those who ask; therefore I pray that my delight would be in Your law. May I meditate on it day and night. Teach me what it is to serve You with fear and rejoice with trembling.

O LORD, be a shield about me, my glory, and the lifter of my head. Assist me to put my trust in You so that my heart exults, saying, "You have put more joy in my heart than they have when their grain and wine abound." In peace make me both lie down and sleep; for You alone, O LORD, make me dwell in safety. Lead me, O LORD, in Your righteousness because of my enemies; make Your way straight before me. Let me take refuge in You and rejoice; let me ever sing for joy, and spread Your protection over me, that I may exult in You as one who loves Your name.

For You bless the righteous, O LORD; You cover me with favor as with a shield. May I give to You the thanks due to Your righteousness, and sing praise to Your Name, Most High.

O my soul, give thanks to the LORD with your whole heart; recount all of His wonderful deeds! Be glad and exult in God; sing praise to His Name, the Most High. For those who know Your Name, O LORD, put their trust in You, for You have not forsaken those who seek You.

Remind me that I am but a mortal, wholly dependent upon You for life and breath and everything else. I commit myself to You. Amen (Psalm 2, 4, 5, 9).

Great I Am,

You are righteous; You love righteous deeds; the upright shall behold Your face. Therefore cause me to walk uprightly so that I might do what I was made for—behold Your wonderful face! May I trust in Your steadfast love; may my heart rejoice in Your salvation. And then let me sing to You, because You have dealt bountifully with me. Again I ask that I be constrained to walk blamelessly and do what is right and speak the truth in my heart.

You are my Lord; I have no good apart from You. You are my chosen portion and my cup; You hold my lot. May I set You always before me; trusting that because You are at my right hand, I shall not be shaken. Please make known to me the path of life; that in Your presence there is fullness of joy; at Your right hand are pleasures evermore.

Wondrously show Your steadfast love to me, O Savior of those who seek refuge from their adversaries at Your right hand. Keep me as the apple of Your eye; hide me in the shadow of Your wings. As for me, may I behold Your face in righteousness; when I awake, may I be satisfied with Your likeness. Praise the LORD! (Psalm 11, 13, 16, 17).

*No prayer is more powerful than the prayer of powerlessness, of littleness, of not knowing. Isn't this what it means to be poor in spirit?* ~Mike Mason

O triune God,

I love You, O LORD, my strength. You are my rock and my fortress and my deliverer, my God, my rock, in whom I take refuge, my shield, and the horn of my salvation, my stronghold. You alone are worthy to be praised.

By Your mercy bring me out into a broad place; rescue me, because You delight in me. Put all Your rules before me, and may I never put Your statutes away from me. For it is You who light my lamp; O LORD my God, lighten my darkness. Make me abide in this precious promise: "This God—His way is perfect; the word of the LORD proves true; He is a shield for all those who take refuge in Him."

Give me the shield of Your salvation, and with Your right hand support me, and with Your gentleness make me great. With Your perfect law, O LORD, revive my soul. With Your sure testimony make me wise. By Your right precepts cause my heart to rejoice. And may Your pure commandment enlighten my eyes.

Keep me, Your servant, also from presumptuous sins; let them not have dominion over me! Let the words of my mouth and the meditation of my heart be pleasing in Your sight, O LORD, my Rock and my Redeemer (Psalm 18 & 19).

*Martin Luther was adamant that we must never get "beyond" God's words in the Bible or we can't know whom we are conversing with. "We must first hear the Word, and then afterwards the Holy Ghost works in our hearts; he works in the hearts of whom he will, and how he will, but never without the Word." ~Tim Keller*

Infinite Father,

It is my plea by the Name of Christ, that You hear me. Since I am one of Your holy and beloved chosen, then put on me compassion, kindness, humility, meekness, and patience. And if one has a complaint against me, let me forgive as You have forgiven me. And above all these put on me love, which binds everything together in perfect harmony.

And let the peace of Christ rule in my heart, to which indeed I was called. And may I be thankful. Let the word of Christ dwell in me richly, as I teach and admonish others in all wisdom, singing psalms and hymns and spiritual songs, with thankfulness in my heart to You. And whatever I do, in word or deed, may everything be in the Name of the Lord Jesus, giving thanks to You, my Father, through Him.

O my soul, continue steadfastly in prayer, being watchful in it with thanksgiving (Colossians 3 & 4).

*How do we structure our adult conversations? We don't. Especially when talking with old friends, the conversation bounces from subject to subject. It has a fun, meandering, play-like quality. Why would our prayer time be any different? After all, God is a person.* ~Paul Miller

All-sufficient King,

May You answer me in the day of trouble! May Your great Name, God of Jacob, protect me! Grant my heart's desire and fulfill all my plans! May I shout for joy over Your salvation, and in the name of my God set up my banners! May You fulfill all my petitions.

Some trust in chariots and some in horses, but let me trust in the name of the LORD my God. Make me glad with the joy of Your presence. Be exalted, O LORD, in Your strength! Let me sing and praise Your power.

When trouble is near and there is none to help, be not far from me. For You, O LORD, are my shepherd; I shall not want. Please make me to lie down in green pastures. Lead me beside still waters. Restore my soul. And by grace, lead me in paths of righteousness for Your Name's sake.

Even when I walk through the valley of the shadow of death, let me fear no evil, for You are with me; with Your rod and Your staff comfort me. May goodness and mercy follow me all the days of my life, that I may dwell in Your house forever (Psalm 20 & 23).

---

*For my part, if I cannot pray, I would rather know it, and groan over my soul's barrenness till the Lord shall again visit me with fruitfulness of devotion.* ~Charles Spurgeon

Life-giving God,

O that I would have clean hands and a pure heart! Guard me so that I do not lift up my soul to what is false or swear deceitfully. Guide me so that I might receive blessings from You and righteousness from the God of my salvation. Cause me to seek You, to seek the face of the God of Jacob.

To You, O LORD, I lift up my soul. O my God, in You I trust; let me not be put to shame; let not my enemies exult over me. Make me to know Your ways, O LORD; teach me Your paths. Lead me in Your truth and teach me, for You are the God of my salvation; for You I wait all the day long.

According to Your steadfast love remember me, for the sake of Your goodness, O LORD! Lead me in humility and what is right; teach me Your way. Instruct me in the way You should choose.

Your friendship, O LORD, is for those who fear You, and You make known to them Your covenant. And so I ask importunately that You would fill me with the fear of You so that I might be Your friend.

Cause my eyes to be ever toward You. Turn to me and be gracious to me when I am lonely and afflicted. O guard my soul and deliver me! Let me not be put to shame, for I take refuge in You. May integrity and uprightness preserve me, for I wait for You (Psalm 24 & 25).

Lord of Heaven,

Cause me to walk in integrity. May I trust in You without wavering. Prove me, O LORD, and try me; test my heart and my mind. Manifest Your steadfast love before my eyes that I may walk in Your faithfulness. Redeem me and be gracious to me.

You are my light and my salvation; whom shall I fear? You are the stronghold of my life; of whom shall I be afraid?

O LORD, I love how You have made me Your habitation and a place where Your glory dwells. I pray that I would earnestly say with the psalmist, "One thing have I asked of the LORD, that will I seek after: that I may dwell in the house of the LORD all the days of my life, to gaze upon the beauty of the LORD and to inquire in his temple."

Your face, LORD, do I seek. Hide not Your face from me. Cast me not off; forsake me not, O God of my salvation!

O my soul, wait for the LORD; be strong, and let your heart take courage; wait for the LORD! (Psalm 26 & 27).

*Prayer often avails where everything else fails.* ~R.A. Torrey

Sovereign Commander of the universe,

You are my only true strength and shield; in You may my heart trust and be helped; let my heart exult, and with my song give thanks to You. You are the strength of Your people; be my saving refuge. May You give me strength!

When I am mourning, turn it into dancing; loose my sackcloth and clothe me with gladness, that my glory may sing Your praise and not be silent. O LORD my God, I will give thanks to You forever!

In You, O LORD, may I take refuge; let me never be put to shame; in Your righteousness deliver me! Cause me to rejoice and be glad in Your steadfast love. Make Your face shine on me; save me in Your steadfast love!

O my soul, the LORD preserves the faithful; be strong and let your heart take courage, you who wait for the LORD!

Keep me, Father; I commit myself wholly to Your Hand (Psalm 28, 30, 31).

*In the Bible we discover a real and complex God. If you have a personal relationship with any real person, you will regularly be confused and infuriated by him or her. So, too, you will be regularly confounded by the God you meet in the Scriptures— as well as amazed and comforted. Your prayer must be firmly connected to and grounded in your reading of the Word. This wedding of the Bible and prayer anchors your life down in the real God. ~Tim Keller*

O Fountain of all good,

Instruct me and teach me in the way I should go; counsel me with Your eye upon me.

May Your steadfast love surround me because I trust in You. Make me glad in You; make me rejoice as a righteous one, shouting for joy as one upright in heart!

Let all the earth fear the LORD; let all the inhabitants of the world stand in awe of You! For You spoke, and I came to be; You commanded, and I stand firm. Behold, how good it is that Your eye is on those who fear You, on those who hope in Your steadfast love. O that my soul would wait for You; be my help and my shield. Together, may our hearts be glad in You, because we trust in Your holy Name. Let Your steadfast love, O LORD, be upon us, even as we hope in You.

Cause me to bless You at all times; may Your praise continually be in my mouth. Let me say, "My soul makes its boast in the LORD; let the humble hear and be glad."

O my soul, magnify the LORD, and exalt His Name forever! (Psalm 32, 33, 34).

*A godly man is carried on the wings of delight. He is never so well as when he is praying. He is not forced with fear but fired with love. 'I will make them joyful in my house of prayer' (Isa. 56:7).* ~Thomas Watson

Searcher of hearts,

I want more and more to taste and see that You are good! Blessed is the person who takes refuge in You! Be near to me when I am brokenhearted, saving me when I am crushed in spirit.

Say to my soul, "I am your salvation!" Then my soul will rejoice in You, exulting in Your salvation. May all my bones say, "O LORD, who is like You, delivering the poor from him who is too strong for him, the poor and needy from him who robs him?"

You have seen, O LORD; be not silent! O Lord, be not far from me! Then my tongue shall tell of Your righteousness and of Your praise all the day long.

Make me feast on the abundance of Your house, and give me drink from the river of Your delights. For with You is the fountain of life; in Your light do we see light. O continue Your steadfast love toward me, and Your righteousness to the upright of heart! Let not the foot of arrogance come upon me, nor the hand of the wicked drive me away.

Please fill me with grace daily, that my life might be a fountain of sweet water. Amen (Psalm 34, 35, 36).

O God who hears the prayers of Your children,

Only You can bring me to trust in You and do good; to dwell in the land and befriend faithfulness. Only Your Hand can turn my heart like a stream of water to delight myself in You so that You will give me the desires of my heart.

O my soul, listen to my entreaty: commit your way to the LORD; trust in Him, and He will act. He will bring forth your righteousness as the light, and your justice as the noonday.

Father, let me be still before You and wait patiently for You; not fretting myself over the one who prospers in his way, over the man who carries out evil devices. For my steps are established by You, when You delight in my way; though I fall, I will not be cast headlong, for You uphold my hand.

It is my plea that my soul would take hope in Your words through David: "I have been young, and now am old, yet I have not seen the righteous forsaken or his children begging for bread."

May my mouth utter wisdom, and my tongue speak justice. May the law of my God be in my heart so that my steps do not slip (Psalm 37).

*Necessity!—I hardly like to talk of that, let me rather speak of the deliciousness of prayer—the wondrous sweetness and divine felicity which come to the soul that lives in the atmosphere of prayer. John Fox said, "The time we spend with God in secret is the sweetest time, and the best improved. Therefore, if thou lovest thy life, be in love with prayer." The devout Mr. Hervey resolved on the bed of sickness—"If God shall spare my life, I will read less and pray more." John Cooke, of Maidenhead, wrote— "The business, the pleasure, the honour, and advantage of prayer press on my spirit with increasing force every day." A deceased pastor when drawing near his end, exclaimed, "I wish I had prayed more"; that wish many of us might utter.*
~Charles Spurgeon

Lord of the cloud and fire,

My salvation is from You; You are my stronghold in the time of trouble. You help me and deliver me; please deliver me from the wicked and save me, because I take refuge in You.

Do not forsake me, O Lord! O my God, be not far from me! Make haste to help me, O Lord, my salvation!

O Lord, make me know my end and what is the measure of my days; let me know how fleeting I am! Behold, You have made my days a few handbreadths, and my lifetime is as nothing before You. Surely all mankind stands as a mere breath!

Hear my prayer—may I wait patiently for You; incline to me and hear my cry. Draw me up from the pit of destruction, out of the miry bog, and set my feet upon a rock, making my steps secure. Put a new song in my mouth, a song of praise to my God. May many see me and fear, and put their trust in You.

Blessed is the man who makes the Lord his trust. As for You, O Lord, do not restrain Your mercy from me; Your steadfast love and Your faithfulness will ever preserve me!

O my soul, hope in God! (Psalm 37, 39, 40).

O God most high, most glorious,

Be pleased to deliver me! O LORD, make haste to help me! Let those be put to shame and disappointed altogether who seek to snatch away my life.

But may I seek You and rejoice and be glad in You; may I love Your salvation and say continually, "Great is the LORD!" You are my help and my deliverer; do not delay, O my God!

As the deer pants for flowing streams, so may my soul pant for You. May my soul thirst for God, for the living God.

When my soul is cast down and in turmoil within me, let me hope in You and praise You—my salvation and my God. By day You command Your steadfast love, and at night may Your song be with me, a prayer to the God of my life.

Send out Your light and Your truth; let them lead me; let them bring me to Your dwelling! Then take me to Your altar; let me delight in You as my exceeding joy and praise You with the lyre, O God, my God.

Why are you cast down, O my soul, and why are you in turmoil within me? Hope in God; for I shall again praise Him, my salvation and my God (Psalm 40, 42, 43).

*Only he who is himself secure and happy in the Lord can pray effectively for others.* ~Mike Mason

Eternal Giver of Life,

May I boast continually in You, and give thanks to Your Name forever. Please redeem me for the sake of Your steadfast love! Be my refuge and strength, a very present help in trouble, so that I may not fear though the earth gives way, though the mountains be moved into the heart of the sea.

O God, be near me so that I will not be moved; help me when morning dawns. Make me to be still and know that You are God. And then let me clap my hands, shouting to You with loud songs of joy!

Know, my soul, that the LORD, the Most High, is to be feared, a great king over all the earth. Sing praises to God, sing praises! Sing praises to our King, sing praises! For God is the King of all the earth; sing praises with a psalm!

Cause me to think on Your steadfast love, O God. Your praise reaches to the ends of the earth. Your right hand is filled with righteousness. Let me be glad! Let me rejoice because of Your judgments! Ransom my soul from the power of Sheol, and shine forth in all Your splendor (Psalm 46, 47, 48, 49).

O Living God,

Incline my heart to offer You a sacrifice of thanksgiving. Have mercy on me according to Your steadfast love; according to Your abundant mercy blot out my transgressions. Wash me thoroughly from my iniquity, and cleanse me from my sin! Make me know my transgressions and in humility have my sin ever before me.

Purge me with hyssop, and I shall be clean; wash me, and I shall be whiter than snow. Let me hear joy and gladness; let the bones that You have broken rejoice. Hide Your face from my sins, and blot out all my iniquities. Create in me a clean heart, O God, and renew a right spirit within me.

Cast me not away from Your presence, and take not Your Holy Spirit from me. Restore unto me the joy of Your salvation, and uphold me with a willing spirit. Then my tongue will sing aloud of Your righteousness. O Lord, open my lips, so that my mouth will declare Your praise.

O my soul, the sacrifices of God are a broken spirit; a broken and contrite heart He will not despise (Psalm 50 & 51).

---

*Why are we called "adulteresses" in praying for something to spend on our pleasures? Because God is our husband and the "world" is a prostitute luring us to give affections to me that belong only to God. This is how subtle the sin of worldliness can be. It can emerge not only against prayer, but in prayer—and fasting. We begin to pray and fast—even intensely—not for God as our all-satisfying husband, but only for his gifts in the world so that we can make love with them.* ~John Piper

Holy LORD,

Make me trust in Your steadfast love forever and ever. May I thank You forever, because You are saving me. O that I would wait for Your Name, for it is good.

Save me, by Your Name, and vindicate me by Your might. O God, hear my prayer; give ear to the words of my mouth. Hide not Yourself from my plea for mercy! Sustain me as I cast my burden upon You; when I am afraid let me trust in You.

In You, whose word I praise, in You I trust; I shall not be afraid. What can flesh do to me? This I know, that You are *for* me.

O my soul, do not be afraid, for what can man do to you? God is *for* you! You need not fear.

Deliver my soul from death, yes, my feet from falling, that I may walk before You in the light of life. Be merciful to me, O God, be merciful to me, for in You my soul takes refuge; in the shadow of Your wings let me take refuge, till the storms of destruction pass by.

Fulfill Your purpose for me and be exalted above the heavens. Let Your glory be over all the earth!

O my soul, sing and make melody! I give thanks to You, O Lord, among the peoples; I will sing praises to You among the nations. For Your steadfast love is great to the heavens, Your faithfulness to the clouds (Psalm 52, 54, 56, 57).

O Changeless God,

Deliver me from my enemies; protect me from those who rise up against me. Then I shall sing of Your strength; make me sing aloud of Your steadfast love in the morning. For You have been to me a fortress and a refuge in the day of my distress. O my strength, I will sing praises to You, for You, O God, are my fortress, the God who shows me steadfast love.

Hear my cry, listen to my prayer; from the end of the earth may I call to You when my heart is faint. Lead me to the rock that is higher than I, for You are a refuge, a strong tower against the enemy. Let me dwell in Your tent forever! Let me take refuge under the shelter of Your wings! Appoint steadfast love and faithfulness to watch over me!

May I wait for You alone in silence; from You comes salvation. You alone must be my rock and my salvation, my fortress; let me not be greatly shaken. My hope must come from You.

Trust in Him at all times, my soul; pour out your heart before Him; God is a refuge for us. Amen (Psalm 59, 61, 62).

---

*You don't create intimacy; you make room for it. This is true whether you are talking about your spouse, your friend, or God. You need space to be together. Efficiency, multitasking, and busyness all kill intimacy. In short, you can't get to know God on the fly.* ~Paul Miller

My Father,

May I earnestly seek You; might my soul thirst for You; make my flesh faint for You, as in a dry and weary land where there is no water. Let me look upon You continually, beholding Your power and glory. Because Your steadfast love is better than life, my lips will praise You.

Form me into a person who will bless You as long as I live, lifting up my hands in Your Name. Satisfy my soul as with fat and rich food. And I ask that I remember You even upon my bed, and meditate on You in the watches of the night, my mouth praising You with joyful lips. For You have been my help, and in the shadow of Your wings I will sing for joy.

O my soul, cling to God, for His right hand upholds you! (Psalm 63).

*How, then, do you pray? Do you ask God for your daily bread? Do you thank God for your conversion? Do you pray for the conversion of others? If the answer is 'no', I can only say that I do not think you are yet born again. But if the answer is 'yes'— well, that proves that, whatever side you may have taken in debates on this question in the past, in your heart you believe in the sovereignty of God no less firmly than anyone else. On our feet we may have arguments about it, but on our knees we are all agreed. ~J.I. Packer*

Lord and King,

Let me rejoice in You and take refuge in You! Let my heart be upright and exult! Praise is due to You, O God—You who hear prayers. Blessed is the one You choose and bring near, to dwell in Your courts! Please secure my place among such chosen.

Shout for joy to God, O my soul; sing the glory of His Name; give to Him glorious praise! Say to God, "How awesome are Your deeds! So great is Your power that Your enemies come cringing to You. All the earth worships You and sings praises to You; they sing praises to Your Name."

May I rejoice in You, who rule by Your might forever. Test me and try me as silver is tried. Please do not reject my prayer or remove Your steadfast love from me! Instead be gracious to me and bless me and make Your face shine upon me, that Your way may be known on earth, Your saving power among all the nations. May I be glad, exulting before You, jubilant with joy! (Psalm 64, 66, 68).

God of Grace,

Thank You that You will bring the good work You began in me to completion at the day of Christ Jesus. It is my prayer that my love may abound more and more, with knowledge and all discernment, so that I may approve what is excellent, and so be pure and blameless for the day of Christ, filled with the fruit of righteousness that comes through Jesus Christ, to the glory and praise of Your name.

I ask that You would enable me to count whatever gain I have as loss for the sake of Christ. Indeed, make me count everything as loss because of the surpassing worth of knowing Christ Jesus my Lord. May I gladly suffer the loss of all things and count them as rubbish, in order that I may gain Christ and be found in Him, not having a righteousness of my own that comes from the law, but that which comes through faith in Christ, the righteousness from You that depends on faith—that I may *know* Christ and the power of His resurrection, and may share in His sufferings, becoming like Him in His death (Philippians 1 & 3).

※

*Our prayers should arise out of immersion in the Scripture. We should "plunge ourselves into the sea" of God's language, the Bible. We should listen, study, think, reflect, and ponder the Scriptures until there is an answering response in our hearts and minds. It may be one of shame or of joy or of confusion or of appeal— but that response to God's speech is then truly prayer and should be given to God.* ~Tim Keller

Almighty God,

Be to me a rock of refuge, to which I may continually come. For You, O Lord, are my hope.

May my mouth be filled with Your praise, and with Your glory all the day. O God, be not far from me; O my God, make haste to help me! May I hope continually and praise You yet more and more. Let my mouth tell of Your righteous acts, of Your deeds of salvation all the day, for their number is past knowledge.

So even to old age and gray hairs, O God, do not forsake me, until I proclaim Your might to another generation, Your power to all those to come (Psalm 71).

*Among all the formative influences which go to make up a man honoured of God in the ministry, I know of none more mighty than his own familiarity with the mercy-seat. All that a college course can do for a student is coarse and external compared with the spiritual and delicate refinement obtained by communion with God. While the unformed minister is revolving upon the wheel of preparation, prayer is the tool of the great potter by which he moulds the vessel. All our libraries and studies are mere emptiness compared with our closets. We grow, we wax mighty, we prevail in private prayer.*
~Charles Spurgeon

Blessed be the LORD, the God of Israel, who alone does wondrous things.

Blessed be Your glorious Name forever; may the whole earth be filled with Your glory!

May I be continually with You—may You hold my right hand. Guide me with Your counsel, for it is perfect, wise, and good. Whom have I in heaven but You? And there is nothing on earth that I desire besides You. I know that my heart and my flesh may fail, therefore be the strength of my heart and my portion forever.

As for me, it is good for me to be near You; let me make You my refuge, that I may tell of all Your works. Continue to mold me into a person who fears You, for who can stand before You once Your anger is roused?

O my soul, remember the deeds of the LORD; yes, remember His wonders of old. Ponder all His work, and meditate on His mighty deeds.

Your way, O God, is holy. What god is great like my God? You are the God who works wonders; You have made known Your might among the peoples. Please work wonders on my behalf, and with Your arm redeem me (Psalm 72, 73, 76, 77).

God of peace,

It is my request that I would set my hope in You and not forget Your works, but keep Your commandments. Let me not be like this stubborn and rebellious generation, a generation whose heart is not steadfast, whose spirit is not faithful to You. Make my heart steadfast toward You and faithful to Your covenant. Thank You for being compassionate, atoning for my iniquity, and not destroying me; You restrained Your anger from me and did not stir up all Your wrath.

Remember that I am but flesh, a wind that passes and comes not again. Restore me, O God of hosts; let Your face shine, that I may be saved!

O my soul, call to Him who alone is your salvation! With all your might seek His wonderful, matchless face! (Psalm 78 & 80).

*God has designed not only that prayer come to be, but that prayer sometimes be a necessary means for accomplishing the ends he has ordained. In other words, God purposely designed how things would work so that some of what he accomplishes can only be accomplished as people pray.* ~Bruce Ware

Blessed Father,

I need to need You. Oh that my soul would long, yes, faint for Your courts; that my heart and flesh would sing for joy to You, the living God. Give me a thankful heart, ever singing Your praise! Bless me with a grateful soul, exalting Your Name forever.

O my soul, sing aloud to God your strength; shout for joy to the God of Jacob! Raise a song; sound the tambourine, the sweet lyre with the harp.

LORD God of hosts, hear my prayer; give ear, O God of Jacob! Bring me into Your presence, for a day in Your courts is better than a thousand elsewhere. May I rather be a doorkeeper in Your house than dwell in the tents of wickedness.

Be my sun and my shield; bestow on me favor and honor. Withhold no good thing from me, because I walk uprightly. O LORD of hosts, blessed is the one who trusts in You! (Psalm 84).

༺❀༻

*What do I lose when I have a praying life? Control. Independence. What do I gain? Friendship with God. A quiet heart. The living work of God in the hearts of those I love. The ability to roll back the tide of evil. Essentially, I lose my kingdom and get his. I move from being an independent player to a dependent lover. I move from being an orphan to a child of God.*
~Paul Miller

O Giving God,

Be gracious to me, for to You do I cry all the day. Gladden the soul of Your servant, for to You, O Lord, do I lift up my soul.

Teach me Your way that I may walk in Your truth; unite my heart to fear Your Name. Turn to me and be gracious to me; give me strength, and save me.

O my soul, sing with me of the steadfast love of the LORD forever; with your mouth make known His faithfulness to all generations!

Make me walk in the light of Your face, exulting in Your Name all the day, exalted in Your righteousness. Teach me to number my days that I may get a heart of wisdom. Satisfy me in the morning with Your steadfast love, that I may rejoice and be glad all my days. Make me glad for the days You have afflicted me, and for as many years as I have seen evil. Let Your work be shown to me, and Your glorious power to my children. Amen (Psalm 86 & 89).

Glorious God,

Let Your favor be upon me. Establish the work of my hands.

Be my dwelling place, Most High, and be my refuge, so that no evil shall be allowed to befall me. Command Your angels concerning me to guard me in all my ways. Because You hold fast to me in love, please deliver me; protect me because I know Your Name.

When I call to You, answer me; be with me in trouble; rescue me and honor me. With long life satisfy me, and show me Your salvation. Satisfy me with Your beauty.

Hear, my soul, while I admonish you! Listen to me: there shall be no strange god before you; you shall not bow down to a foreign god. Go to the LORD! Open your mouth wide, and He will fill it. He will feed you with the finest of wheat, and with honey from the rock He will satisfy you (Psalm 90, 91, 81).

*Prayer is the process of crouching down and making ourselves small before God. This downsizing is not an option; it is the only way to enter the kingdom of heaven. To grow in the Spirit is to become little in relation to more and more areas of life—marriage, family, church, work—until eventually it is possible to be little and childlike even in the presence of Satan and all his demons. For it is God, not you or I, who is bigger than evil.*
~Mike Mason

Faithful Creator,

Thank you for the grace and peace that has been multiplied to me in the knowledge of You and of Jesus our Lord. May I grow in the grace and knowledge of our Lord and Savior Jesus Christ. When I suffer according to Your will, let me entrust my soul to a faithful Creator while doing good.

Let me not love the world or the things in the world, and may I keep myself from idols.

O my soul, do not love what is passing away more than your God! Instead build yourself up in your most holy faith; pray in the Holy Spirit; keep yourself in the love of God, waiting for the mercy of your Lord Jesus Christ that leads to eternal life.

Now to You who are able to keep me from stumbling and to present me blameless before the presence of Your glory with great joy, to the only God, my Savior, through Jesus Christ my Lord, be glory, majesty, dominion, and authority, before all time and now and forever. Amen (II Peter 3, I John 2, Jude).

Glorious and Holy God,

You have made me glad by Your work; at the works of Your hands I sing for joy. How great are Your works, O LORD! Your thoughts are very deep! Therefore keep me in Your care, and discipline me, and teach me out of Your law. For blessed is the person whom You discipline, to give them rest from days of trouble. Do not forsake me or abandon me as Your heritage.

If You are not my help, my soul would soon live in the land of silence. When my foot slips, hold me up, O LORD, with Your steadfast love. When the cares of my heart are many, cheer my soul with Your consolations. Become my stronghold, and my rock of refuge.

O my soul, sing to the LORD; make a joyful noise to the rock of your salvation! Come into His presence with thanksgiving; make a joyful noise to Him with songs of praise! For You, O LORD, are a great God, and a great King above all gods (Psalm 92, 94, 95).

※

*If we do not learn to pray, it will not be for want of instructions and examples. Look at Abraham, taking it upon him to speak unto the Lord for Sodom. Look at Isaac, who goes out to meditate in the field at the eventide. Look at Jacob, as he wrestles until the breaking of the day at the Jabbok. Look at Hannah, as she speaks in her heart. Look at David, as he prevents now the dawning of the day, and now the watches of the night, in a hundred psalms. Look at our Lord. And then, look at Paul, as great in prayer as he is in preaching, or in writing Epistles. No, –if you never learn to pray, it will not be for want of the clearest instructions, and the most shining examples. ~Alexander Whyte*

Lord Christ,

Only by Your blood and imputed righteousness do I approach the Father with confidence. Therefore, Father, as I received Christ Jesus the Lord, may I so walk in Him, rooted and built up in Him and established in the faith, just as I was taught, abounding in thanksgiving.

O my soul, if then you have been raised with Christ, seek the things that are above, where Christ is, seated at the right hand of God. Set your mind on things that are above, not on things that are on earth. For you have died, and your life is hidden with Christ in God.

Father, help me to walk in my new self, which is being renewed in knowledge after the image of its creator. Assist me to put to death what is earthly in me: sexual immorality, impurity, passion, evil desire, and covetous-ness, which is idolatry. Let me put them all away: anger, wrath, malice, slander, and obscene talk from my mouth. You are the great healer and refiner. Purify me by whatever means are necessary. Make me wholly Yours. Amen (Colossians 2 & 3).

Lord God Almighty,

Grant that I declare Your glory among the nations; Your marvelous works among all the peoples. For great are You Lord, and greatly to be praised; You are to be feared above all gods. Splendor and majesty are before You; strength and beauty are in Your sanctuary.

May I ascribe to You glory and strength! Let me ascribe to You the glory due Your Name, worshiping You in the splendor of holiness. Make me say among the nations, "The Lord reigns!"

Let me hear of Your righteousness and be glad, rejoicing with the daughters of Judah because of Your judgments, O Lord. May I hate evil, for You preserve the lives of Your saints; You deliver them from the hand of the wicked.

O my soul come, worship and bow down; kneel before the Lord, your Maker! For He is your God, and you are one of the people of His pasture, and the sheep of His hand (Psalm 96 & 95).

---

*Resolved, never to count that a prayer, nor to let that pass as a prayer, nor that as a petition of a prayer, which is so made, that I cannot hope that God will answer it; nor that as a confession, which I cannot hope God will accept.*
~Jonathan Edwards

Eternal Father,

With Your right hand and Your holy arm please work salvation for me. Remember Your steadfast love and faithfulness to Your children so that all the ends of the earth will see the salvation of my God.

Make a joyful noise to the LORD, my soul; break forth into joyous song and sing praises! Join with the sea as it roars, with the world and those who dwell in it, with the rivers as they clap their hands, with the hills singing for joy together before the LORD.

O God, may I ponder the way that is blameless, and walk in integrity of heart. Let me not set before my eyes anything that is worthless, keeping a perverse heart far from me.

Do not hide Your face from me in the day of my distress! Incline Your ear to me; answer speedily when I call! And by Your infinite mercy grant my heart to pour forth in song, "Bless the LORD, O my soul, and all that is within me, bless His holy Name" (Psalm 98, 102, 103).

*It is crucial that we not be more fascinated, more gripped, by the prayers of a man than by the pleasures of God. How easy it is to be more thrilled by radical devotion than by divine beauty.*
~John Piper

Bless the LORD, O my soul!

O LORD my God, You are very great! You are clothed with splendor and majesty, covering Yourself with light as with a garment. And by the blood and mercy of Your perfect Son I appeal to Your wise power.

May my meditation be pleasing to You, for I rejoice in You. Let me thank You for Your steadfast love, for Your wondrous works to the children of men! Satisfy my longing soul; when my soul hungers fill it with good things. Send out Your word and heal me, and deliver me from destruction. Let me sing and make melody with all my being!

Awake, my soul! Awake the dawn! Give thanks to the LORD among the peoples; sing praises to Him among the nations. For Your steadfast love, O God, is above the heavens; Your faithfulness reaches to the clouds. Be exalted, O God, above the heavens! Let Your glory be over me! Amen (Psalm 104, 107, 108).

*God's Word enabled David to "find the heart [Hebrew leb] to pray this prayer to you." The Word of God created within David the desire, drive, and strength to pray. The principle: God speaks to us in his Word, and we respond in prayer, entering into the divine conversation, into communion with God.*
~Tim Keller

O LORD,

Grant me help against the foe, for vain is the salvation of man! With You I shall do valiantly. O GOD my Lord, deal on my behalf for Your Name's sake; because Your steadfast love is good, deliver me! With my mouth let me give great thanks to You, praising You in the midst of sorrow. For You stand at the right hand of the needy, to save me from those who condemn my soul to death.

Praise be to You, LORD! I will give thanks to You with my whole heart, in the company of the upright, in the congregation. Great are Your works, studied by all who delight in them. Therefore help me to study them diligently. Be exalted, for Your work is full of splendor and majesty.

Show me the power of Your works—that they are faithful and just; all Your precepts are trustworthy; they are established forever and ever, to be performed with faithfulness and uprightness.

O my soul, fear the LORD, for it is the beginning of wisdom; all those who practice this fear have a good understanding. His praise endures forever! (Psalm 108, 109, 111).

O Divine Comforter,

When I sow in tears, let me reap with shouts of joy. Grant me assurance in the God of my salvation, hoping in You and Your steadfast love.

May I wait for You, and hope in Your word. Continually make me into a person whose soul waits for You more than watchmen for the morning.

O my soul, hope in the LORD! For with the LORD there is steadfast love, and with Him is plentiful redemption. Hope in the LORD from this time forth and forevermore.

I praise You, LORD, for You are good; I sing to Your Name for it is pleasant! For You have chosen me for Yourself; I am Your own possession. Do as You please with me; deal with me according to Your sovereign purpose. For I know that You are great, and that You are above all gods (Psalm 126, 130, 128, 135).

*True religion makes us want to spend time alone in meditation and prayer. We read that this was true for Isaac (Gen. 24:63). Even more important, we read in the Gospels that Christ too needed to be alone with His Father. Concealing deep feeling is difficult, and yet grace-filled feeling is often more silent and private than that which is counterfeit.* ~Jonathan Edwards

Living God,

Remember me even in my low estate, for Your steadfast love endures forever. Though I walk in the midst of trouble, preserve my life; stretch out Your hand against the wrath of my enemies and deliver me. Please fulfill Your purposes for me; Your steadfast love, O LORD, endures forever. Do not forsake the work of Your hands.

O LORD, search me and know me! Hem me in, behind and before, and lay Your hand upon me.

I praise You, for I am fearfully and wonderfully made. Wonderful are Your works; my soul knows it very well. My frame was not hidden from You, when I was being made in secret, intricately woven in the depths of the earth. Your eyes saw my unformed substance; in Your book were written, every one of them, the days that were formed for me, when as yet there were none of them.

Therefore take confidence, my soul! The Almighty LORD of heaven and earth will accomplish for you what is best. Faint not; be not downcast but sleep in His gracious providence, for when you awake He is still with you (Psalm 138 & 139).

*I myself have seen this rare beauty on the face of a young woman at prayer, one who most likely had no idea that she was being seen by human eyes. Her countenance was incomparably more lovely than anything Hollywood's cosmetology is able to achieve. Indeed, divine grace working in a receptive soul does produce what St. Paul calls "God's work of art" (Eph 2:10).*
~Thomas Dubay

Author of Salvation,

Make me ready to share with others not only the gospel of God but also my own self. May You and the Lord Jesus direct my way, and make me increase and abound in love for all, so that You may establish my heart blameless in holiness before Yourself at the coming of our Lord Jesus with all His saints.

Make me worthy of Your calling and may I fulfill every resolve for good and every work of faith by Your power, so that the Name of the Lord Jesus may be glorified in me, and me in Him, according to Your grace and the grace of the Lord Jesus Christ.

I ought always to give thanks to You, because You chose me to be saved, through sanctification by the Spirit and belief in the truth.

O my soul, to this He called you through the gospel, so that you may obtain the glory of the Lord Jesus Christ. So then, stand firm and hold to the traditions that you were taught by His word.

Now may the Lord Jesus Christ Himself, and You, Father, who loved me and gave me eternal comfort and good hope through grace, comfort my heart and establish it in every good work and word. Amen (I Thessalonians 3 & II Thessalonians 1 & 2).

God of hosts,

Restore me; let Your face shine, that I may be saved! Search me, O God, and know my heart. Try me and know my thoughts. And see if there be any grievous way in me, and lead me in the way everlasting.

Set a guard, O LORD, over my mouth; keep watch over the door of my lips! Do not let my heart incline to any evil, to busy myself with wicked deeds. Let a righteous word strike me—it is a kindness; let it rebuke me—it is oil for my head; let my head not refuse it.

May I cry out to You, O LORD and say, "You are my refuge, my portion in the land of the living." Attend to my cry, especially when I am brought very low.

Cause me to remember the days of old, meditate on all that You have done, and ponder the work of Your hands. Let me stretch out my hands to You when my soul thirsts for You like a parched land. Hide not Your face from me, lest I be like those who go down to the pit.

Let me hear in the morning of Your steadfast love, for in You I trust. Make me know the way I should go, for to You I lift up my soul. Amen (Psalm 80, 141, 142, 143).

*If you are not praying, then you are quietly confident that time, money, and talent are all you need in life. You'll always be a little too tired, a little too busy. But if, like Jesus, you realize you can't do life on your own, then no matter how busy, no matter how tired you are, you will find the time to pray.* ~Paul Miller

Radiant Redeemer,

Teach me to do Your will, for You are my God! Let Your good Spirit lead me on level ground! For Your Name's sake, O LORD, preserve my life! In Your righteousness bring my soul out of trouble.

I confess that I deserve none of these mercies, but only death and wrath. For what is man that You regard him, or the son of man that You think of him? Man is like a breath; his days are like a passing shadow. But praise be to You, Christ Jesus, for Your righteous obedience and perfect atonement.

O my soul, do you know His greatness? He is great and greatly to be praised, and His greatness is unsearchable. Extol Him as your God and King. Every day bless Him and praise His name forever and ever.

Grant, Lord God, that I be a person who meditates on the glorious splendor of Your majesty and on Your wondrous works. A person who speaks of the might of Your awesome deeds, and declares Your greatness. A person who pours forth the fame of Your abundant goodness and sings aloud of Your righteousness. Amen (Psalm 143, 144, 145).

*The magnificence of God is the source and measure of the magnificence of prayer. "Think magnificently of God."*
~Alexander Whyte

King of Kings,

I appeal to Your testimony concerning Yourself: that You are gracious and merciful, slow to anger and abounding in steadfast love. You are good to all, and Your mercy is over all that You have made. Therefore, be eternally kind towards me. Keep me in the love of Christ, and let me give thanks to You and bless You always.

May I speak of the glory of Your kingdom and tell of Your power. Let me make known to the children of man Your mighty deeds, and the glorious splendor of Your kingdom. For Your kingdom is an everlasting kingdom, and Your dominion endures throughout all generations.

My soul, know this God! He is righteous in all His ways and kind in all His works. Trust this God, for He is near to all who call on Him, to all who call on Him in truth. Love this God, for He fulfills the desire of those who fear Him, and preserves all who love Him.

Let my mouth speak Your praise, O LORD, and let all flesh bless Your holy Name forever and ever (Psalm 145).

*In our Lord's prayer, he told us to pray, "Your kingdom come, your will be done, on earth as it is in heaven" (Matt. 6:10). This indicates that the perfect will of God precedes my praying and yours. We are not told to pray, "your will be formed," but "your will be done."* ~Bruce Ware

Prince of Peace,

I will praise You as long as I live; I will sing praises to my God while I have being. Let me be glad in my Maker, rejoicing in my King! Let me praise Your Name with dancing, making melody to You with my voice. Please take pleasure in my song and adorn me with salvation.

Let me exult in glory; let me sing for joy on my bed. Let Your high praises be in my throat and Your word in my hands. May I praise You in Your sanctuary; praise You in Your mighty heavens! Make me praise You for Your mighty deeds; praise You according to Your excellent greatness!

Put not your trust in princes, my soul, in a son of man, in whom there is no salvation. But blessed is he whose help is the God of Jacob, whose hope is in the LORD his God, who made heaven and earth, the sea, and all that is in them, who keeps faith forever; who executes justice for the oppressed, who gives food to the hungry.

Everything that has breath praise the LORD! Praise the LORD! (Psalm 146, 149, 150).

Wise Counselor,

I ask that I would hear Your instruction and not forsake Your teaching, for they are a graceful garland for my head and pendants for my neck. All good things come from You, O God, therefore make my ear attentive to wisdom and incline my heart to understanding; yes, let me call out for insight and raise my voice for understanding, seeking it like silver and searching for it as for hidden treasures. Give me such fervor so that I might understand the fear of You and find the knowledge of God.

Let not steadfast love and faithfulness forsake me; bind them around my neck; write them on the tablet of my heart.

Trust in the LORD with all your heart, my soul! And lean not on your own understanding. In all your ways acknowledge Him, and He will make straight your paths. Be not wise in your own eyes; fear the LORD, and turn away from evil.

Lord God, may I honor You with my wealth and with the firstfruits of all my produce; then my barns will be filled with plenty, and my vats will be bursting with wine. Let me not despise Your discipline or be weary of Your reproof, for You reprove those whom You love, as a father the children in whom he delights (Proverbs 1, 2, 3).

*Better be somewhat too bold and somewhat unseemly than altogether to neglect and forget Almighty God. Better say that so bold saying, —"I will not let Thee go," than pray with such laziness and sleepiness and stupidity as we now pray.*
*~Alexander Whyte*

Father of our Lord Jesus,

May You direct my heart to Your love and to the steadfastness of Christ. Work this miracle of grace in me: that I would count it all joy when I meets trials of various kinds.

If I lack wisdom, let me ask You, who give generously to all without reproach, so that it will be given me. Cause me to be a doer of the word, and not a hearer only, so that I might not deceive myself.

Though I have not seen You, let me love You. Though I do not now see You, let me believe in You and rejoice with joy that is inexpressible and filled with glory, obtaining the outcome of my faith, the salvation of my soul.

O my soul, it is my greatest joy and privilege to remind you that you are of a chosen race, a royal priesthood, a holy nation, a people for God's own possession, that you may proclaim the excellencies of Him who called you out of darkness into His marvelous light. O remember! Once you were an orphan, but now you are God's child; once you had not received mercy, but now you have received mercy!

To You alone, Lord God, be glory forever! Amen (James 1 & I Peter 1 & 2).

# God of Truth,

Please be my confidence, and keep my foot from being caught. May I keep hold of instruction and not let it go; let me guard it, for it is my life. Make me commit my work to You so that my plans may be established.

O my soul, better is a little with the fear of the LORD than great treasure and trouble with it. The fear of the LORD is a fountain of life, that you may turn away from the snares of death.

Father, importunately I ask that I would find wisdom and get understanding, for the gain from it is better than gain from silver and its profit better than gold. May I consider wisdom as more precious than jewels, for long life is in my right hand; in my left hand are riches and honor. Let me not lose sight of these—sound wisdom and discretion, for they will be life for my soul and adornment for my neck (Proverbs 3, 16, 15).

*There is no true prayer without agony. Perhaps this is the problem in many of our churches. What little prayer we have is shallow, timid, carefully censored, and full of oratorical flourishes and hot air. There is little agony in it, and therefore little honesty or humility. We seem to think that the Lord is like everyone else we know, and that He cannot handle real honesty. So we put on our Sunday best to visit Him, and when we return home and take off our fancy duds we are left alone with what is underneath: the dirty underwear of hypocrisy.* ~Mike Mason

Lord and Father,

Thank You for calling me to belong to Jesus Christ. I praise You for loving me and calling me to be among the saints!

Grant that my brothers and sisters and I may be mutually encouraged by each other's faith. And let me never be ashamed of the gospel, for it is the power of God for salvation to everyone who believes. For in it Your righteousness is revealed from faith for faith.

Indeed, when I was outside of Christ I failed to please You; I could not. I was not righteous, and there was no fear of You before my eyes.

O my soul, remember your depravity—the low estate from which He saved you! You have sinned and fallen short of His glory, and are justified by His grace as a gift, through the redemption that is in Christ Jesus, whom God put forward as a propitiation by His blood. And this was to show His righteousness, so that He might be just and the justifier of the one who has faith in Jesus.

Therefore I cannot boast, O LORD, for all that I have is of grace through Christ! May I live and breathe and eat and drink by grace alone, for Your glory alone (Romans 1 & 3).

---

*God has made the spread of his fame hang on the preaching of his Word; and he has made the preaching of his Word hang on the prayers of the saints. This is the awesome place of prayer in the purposes of God for the world. The triumph of the Word will not come without prayer.* ~John Piper

Holy Father,

Your servant David exults by saying, "Blessed are those whose lawless deeds are forgiven, and whose sins are covered." Therefore, please do not count them against me! I know that there will be tribulation and distress for every human being who does evil, and I have been wicked. I have had a hard and impenitent heart, thus storing up wrath for myself on the day of wrath when Your righteous judgment will be revealed. I have dishonored You by breaking Your wonderful law. Your name has been blasphemed among the Gentiles because of me. But thank You that for Your namesake You impute to me the righteousness of Your Son. By Your Holy Spirit keep me trusting in Christ's perfection alone, for You raised Him from the dead for my justification after He had been delivered up for my trespasses.

Therefore, my soul, since you have been justified by faith, you have peace with God through the Lord Jesus Christ! O embrace and kiss Him! For through Him you have also obtained access by faith into this grace in which you stand. Let us, therefore, together rejoice in hope of the glory of God.

More than that, Father, help us to rejoice in our sufferings, knowing that suffering produces endurance, and endurance produces character, and character produces hope, and hope does not put us to shame, because Your love has been poured into our hearts through the Holy Spirit who has been given to us. Amen (Romans 2 & 5).

Incomparable God,

I praise You that while I was still weak and ungodly, Christ died for me. For one will scarcely die for a righteous person, but You have shown Your love for me in that while I was still a sinner, Christ died for me.

O my soul, since therefore you have been justified by His blood, much more shall you be saved by Him from the wrath of God. Rejoice! Rejoice in God through the Lord Jesus Christ, through whom you have now received reconciliation.

Father, let me not continue in sin so that grace may abound. May it never be! Do not allow me to live in sin once I have died to it. Cause me to consider myself dead to sin and alive to You in Christ Jesus. Let not sin reign in my mortal body, to make me obey its passions. Keep me from presenting my members to sin as instruments for unrighteousness. For sin will have no dominion over me, since I am not under law but under grace.

Just as I once presented my members as slaves to impurity and to lawlessness leading to more lawlessness, so now may I present my members as slaves to righteousness leading to sanctification. Instill this truth ever deeply within me: the wages of sin is death, but Your free gift is eternal life in Christ Jesus our Lord. Restrain me from earning deadly wages. And come quickly, Lord Jesus. We long for You. Amen (Romans 5 & 6).

Deliciously Gracious Master,

When I find myself divided in my desires, help me. There will be times when I delight in Your law in my inner being, but I see in my members another law waging war against the law of my mind and making me captive to the law of sin that dwells in my members. And when I cry, "Wretched person that I am! Who will deliver me from this body of death?" make me hope in You through Jesus Christ me Lord!

O my soul, there is now no condemnation for those who are in Christ Jesus. For the law of the Spirit of life has set you free in Christ Jesus from the law of sin and death.

O God, cause me to exult in the knowledge that You have done what the law, weakened by the flesh, could not do. By sending Your own Son in the likeness of sinful flesh and for sin, You condemned sin in the flesh, in order that the righteous requirement of the law might be fulfilled in us who walk not according to the flesh but according to the Spirit. Although my body is dead because of sin, give me life by the Spirit because of righteousness! Amen (Romans 7 & 8).

*Pray often, for prayer is a shield to the soul, a sacrifice to God, and a scourge for Satan.* ~John Bunyan

Abba, Father,

I ask that Your Spirit would bear witness with my spirit that I am Your child. For I did not receive a spirit of slavery to fall back into fear, but You granted me the Spirit of adoption as Your child. Cause me to live according to Your Spirit and not according to the flesh. For if I live according to the flesh I will die, but if by the Spirit I put to death the deeds of the body I will live.

Please be faithful to bear witness with my spirit that I am Your child, and if a child, then an heir—Your heir and fellow heir with Christ, provided I suffer with Him in order that I may also be glorified with Him.

Therefore grant me the grace of strength to consider that the sufferings of this present time are not worth comparing with the glory that is to be revealed to me.

O my soul, be not discouraged when you groan inwardly as you wait eagerly for your adoption, the redemption of your body. For in this hope you were saved. Wait for it with patience.

O LORD, I long for the return of Your beautiful Son. Come quickly, Christ Jesus. Amen (Romans 8).

Beloved God,

By Your Spirit, help me in my weakness. For I do not know what to pray for as I ought, therefore may Your Spirit be faithful to intercede for me with groanings too deep for words. For You, who search hearts, know what is the mind of the Spirit, because the Spirit intercedes for the saints according to Your will.

O my soul, know for certain that for those who love God all things work together for good, for those who are called according to His purpose. For those whom He foreknew he also predestined to be conformed to the image of His Son, in order that He might be the firstborn among many brothers.

Father, thank You for Your sovereign choice; for loving me into faith in Christ, for predestining me to be conformed to His blessed image! Be magnified and lifted high for Your perfect work in me. Amen (Romans 8).

*There is a general kind of praying which fails for lack of precision. It is as if a regiment of soldiers should all fire off their guns anywhere. Possibly somebody would be killed, but the majority of the enemy would be missed.* ~Charles Spurgeon

Almighty Infinite Father,

If You are for me, who can be against me? You who did not spare Your own Son but gave Him up for us all, how will You not also with Him graciously give me all things? Who shall bring any charge against me as Your elect? It is You who justify. Who is to condemn? Assure me with the truth that Christ Jesus is the one who died—more than that, who was raised—who is at Your right hand, who indeed is interceding for me. I praise You that no one shall separate me from the love of Christ. Even tribulation, or distress, or persecution, or famine, or nakedness, or danger, or sword shall not prevail over His love.

Do you trust His grasp, my soul? Do you hope in the triumph of God alone, even when you are killed all the day long and regarded as a sheep to be slaughtered? For in all these things we are more than conquerors through Him who loved us. You can be sure that neither death nor life, nor angels nor rulers, nor things present nor things to come, nor powers, nor height nor depth, nor anything else in all creation, will be able to separate you from the love of God in Christ Jesus our Lord (Romans 8).

*I have been driven many times to my knees by the overwhelming conviction that I had absolutely no other place to go.*
~Abraham Lincoln

Effectual Lover,

Your purpose of election must stand, for it is beautiful and wise to choose a people not because of works but because of Your call. May I learn to rejoice and tremble at Your words, "Jacob I loved, but Esau I hated." Let me not charge You with injustice because You are free. For You say to Moses, "I will have mercy on whom I have mercy, and I will have compassion on whom I have compassion." Thank You that it depends not on human will or exertion, but on You, who have mercy.

Let me love and fear the truth that You have mercy on whomever You will, and You harden whomever You will. Keep me from being a person who questions You with arrogance, or sets my ways of justice above You, or demands You to account for what I find inequitable. May I not question my molder, saying, "Why have You made me like this?" For You are the Lord and potter, and to You belongs the right to make one vessel for honored use and another for dishonorable use.

O my soul, adore His goodness! In order to make known to you the riches of His glory He endured with much patience vessels of wrath prepared for destruction, to show His wrath and to make known His power.

Father, may Your Son be my greatest good forever. Amen (Romans 9).

Great Shepherd of Your sheep,

My heart's desire and prayer is that I may be saved. Let me never be a person who has a zeal for God, but not according to knowledge. Keep me from being ignorant of the righteousness that comes from You, and seeking to establish my own, thus failing to submit to Your righteousness. For Your Son is the end of the law for righteousness to everyone who believes.

Let this assurance ring afresh in my heart: that if I confess with my mouth that Jesus is Lord and believe in my heart that You raised Him from the dead, I will be saved.

O my soul, adore the free goodness of the Lord's salvation! For the Scripture says, "Everyone who believes in Him will not be put to shame." For there is no distinction between Jew and Greek; the same Lord is Lord of all, bestowing His riches on all who call on Him. For "everyone who calls on the name of the Lord will be saved."

Father, You have told us that faith comes through hearing, and hearing through the word of Christ. Therefore use me to proclaim the good news so that my feet might be called beautiful. Amen (Romans 10).

Wise Husbandman,

Thank You for choosing me by grace. And if it is by grace, it is no longer on the basis of works; otherwise grace would no longer be grace. Thank You for sparing me from hardening, from a spirit of stupor, from eyes that cannot see and ears that cannot hear.

Make me humbly grateful that some of the natural branches were broken off, and I, although a wild olive shoot, was grafted in among the others and now share in the nourishing root of the olive tree. Let me never be arrogant toward the branches, remembering that it is not I who support the root, but the root that supports me. Do not allow me to become proud, but cause me to stand in awe. For if You did not spare the natural branches, neither will You spare me.

My soul, note then the kindness and the severity of God: severity toward those who have fallen, but God's kindness to you, provided you continue in His kindness. Otherwise you too will be cut off.

Lord God, lest I be wise in my own conceits, help me to understand this mystery: a partial hardening has come upon Israel, until the fullness of the Gentiles has come in. May I tremble before Your sovereign hand that has consigned all to disobedience, that You may have mercy on all.

Oh, the depth of Your riches and wisdom and knowledge! How unsearchable are Your judgments and how inscrutable Your ways! For who has known Your mind, or who has been Your counselor? Or who has given a gift to You that he might be repaid? For from You and through You and to You are all things. To You be glory forever. Amen (Romans 11).

**M**agnificent God,

I appeal to You by Your mercies, to receive my body as a living sacrifice, holy and acceptable to You. And grant me the willingness to present my body in this way, as my spiritual worship. Let me not be conformed to this world, but transform me by the renewal of my mind, that by testing I may discern what is Your will, what is good and acceptable and perfect.

May I not think of myself more highly than I ought to think, but rather think with sober judgment, according to the measure of faith that You have assigned. Enable me to use my gifts according to the grace given me: if prophecy, in proportion to my faith; if service, in my serving; if I teach, in my teaching; if I exhort, in my exhortation; if I contribute, in generosity; if I lead, with zeal; if I do acts of mercy, with cheerfulness.

O my soul, let your love be genuine. Abhor what is evil; hold fast to what is good. Love with brotherly affection. Seek to outdo others in showing honor. Do not be slothful in zeal, be fervent in spirit, serve the Lord.

Lord God, only by Your sovereign grace will I be able to rejoice in hope, be patient in tribulation, and be constant in prayer. Assist me as I strive to contribute to the needs of the saints and seek to show hospitality. Amen (Romans 12).

*When thou prayest, rather let thy heart be without words, than thy words without a heart.* ~John Bunyan

Awesome LORD,

Only by Your unmerited favor will I grow in likeness to Christ Jesus. So I entreat Your mercy to enable me to bless those who persecute me; to bless and not curse them. Let me rejoice with those who rejoice, weep with those who weep, and live in harmony with my heavenly family. May I not be haughty, but associate with the lowly, giving myself to humble tasks. Let me never be conceited, nor repay anyone evil for evil. Instead grant that I give thought to do what is honorable in the sight of all. If possible, so far as it depends on me, help me live peaceably with all.

O my soul, never avenge yourself, but leave it to the wrath of God, for it is written, "Vengeance is mine, I will repay, says the LORD." To the contrary, if your enemy is hungry, feed him; if he is thirsty, give him something to drink; for by so doing you will heap burning coals on his head.

Holy God, do not let me be overcome by evil, but assist me to overcome evil with good; to cast off the works of darkness and put on the armor of light. Let me walk properly as in the daytime, not in orgies and drunkenness, not in sexual immorality and sensuality, not in quarreling and jealousy. But cause me to put on the Lord Jesus Christ, and make no provision for the flesh, to gratify its desires.

Come, Lord Jesus. I yearn for the day of Your unveiled beauty. Amen (Romans 12 & 13).

O God who is faithful when we are faithless,

Let me not live to myself. If I live, may I live to You, and if I die, may I die to You. So that whether I live or whether I die, I might be Yours. For to this end Christ died and lived again, that He might be Lord both of the dead and of the living.

O my soul, do not pass judgment on your sister, or despise your brother. For we will all stand before the judgment seat of God; for it is written, "As I live, says the Lord, every knee shall bow to me, and every tongue shall confess to God." So then we will both give an account of ourselves to God.

Therefore Father, let me not pass judgment on my brothers and sisters any longer, but rather decide never to put a stumbling block or hindrance in their way. Cause me to pursue what makes for peace and for mutual upbuilding.

Remind me of my obligation as a person of strength to bear with the failings of the weak, and not to please myself.

I ask, for the sake of Your Name, that through endurance and through the encouragement of the Scriptures I might have hope. May You enable me to live in such harmony with others, in accord with Christ Jesus, that we may with one voice glorify You, the God and Father of our Lord Jesus Christ (Romans 14 & 15).

---

*I can think of nothing great that is also easy. Prayer must be, then, one of the hardest things in the world.* ~Tim Keller

**G**od of Hope,

Fill me with all joy and peace in believing, so that by the power of the Holy Spirit I may abound in hope. Fill me also with goodness and with all knowledge, enabling me to instruct others.

I appeal to you, my soul, by our Lord Jesus Christ and by the love of the Spirit, to strive in your prayers to God, that you may be delivered from your propensity to wander from the narrow road, so that by God's will you may serve others with joy and be refreshed in their company.

I appeal to You, Lord God, to give me discernment and vigilance to watch out for those who cause divisions and create obstacles contrary to the doctrine that I have been taught; help me to avoid them. Safeguard me from their smooth talk and flattery by which they deceive the hearts of the naïve. I want me to be wise as to what is good and innocent as to what is evil. Now to You who are able to strengthen me according to the gospel and the preaching of Jesus Christ, according to Your command, to bring about the obedience of faith—to You, the only wise God, be glory forevermore through Jesus Christ! Amen (Romans 15 & 16).

*Pray, and let God worry.* ~Martin Luther

Christ Jesus,

I praise You that in these last days God has spoken to us by You, His Son, whom He appointed heir of all things, through whom also He created the world.

Father, thank You for sending Your Son as the radiance of Your glory and the exact imprint of Your nature, upholding the universe by the word of His power. May I exalt Him as much superior to angels as the name He has inherited is more excellent than theirs.

O my soul, exalt Him, saying, "Your throne, Lord Christ, is forever and ever, the scepter of uprightness is the scepter of Your kingdom. You have loved righteousness and hated wickedness; therefore God, Your God, has anointed You with the oil of gladness beyond Your companions."

You, Lord, laid the foundation of the earth in the beginning, and the heavens are the work of Your hands; they will perish, but You remain; they will all wear out like a garment, like a robe You will roll them up, like a garment they will be changed. But You are the same, and Your years have no end.

Father, cause me to adore Your magnificent Son incessantly and abound in thanksgiving for every glimpse of His beauty.

I long to see Him face to face. Amen (Hebrews 1).

Gracious Father,

May I consider Jesus, the apostle and high priest of my confession, who was faithful to You who appointed Him, just as Moses also was faithful in all Your house. For Jesus has been counted worthy of more glory than Moses—as much more glory as the builder of a house has more honor than the house itself. Now Moses was faithful in all Your house as a servant to testify to the things that were to be spoken later, but Christ is faithful over Your house as a son.

O my soul, you are part of His house if indeed you hold fast your confidence and your boasting in your hope.

Therefore Father, today, if I hear Your voice, let me not harden my heart as in the rebellion. Guard me, lest there be in me an evil, unbelieving heart, leading me to fall away from the living God.

Help me to exhort others every day, as long as it is called "today," that we may not be hardened by the deceitfulness of sin. For I share in Christ, if indeed I hold my original confidence firm to the end. Enable me to endure steadfastly! Enable me so that I might gain Your glorious Son!

Amen, come quickly Lord Jesus (Hebrews 3).

God of the living word,

Only through Christ, the great high priest, who is better than angels and greater than Moses—only through Him do I come to You. I pray that while the promise of entering Your rest still stands I would fear lest I should seem to have failed to reach it. May Your good news meet with faith in me as I hear it.

I praise You that there remains a Sabbath rest for Your people, for whoever has entered Your rest has also rested from their works as You did from Yours. As the Scriptures say, "And God rested on the seventh day from all His works."

Let me therefore strive to enter that rest, so that I may not fall by the same sort of disobedience that overtook all those who left Egypt led by Moses. For Your word is living and active, sharper than any two-edged sword, piercing to the division of soul and of spirit, of joints and of marrow, and discerning the thoughts and intentions of the heart. And no creature is hidden from Your sight, but all are naked and exposed to Your eyes. And to You we must give an account.

O my soul, since you have a great high priest who has passed through the heavens, Jesus, the Son of God, hold fast your confession. For you do not have a high priest who is unable to sympathize with your weaknesses, but one who in every respect has been tempted as you are, yet without sin. Therefore, draw near to the throne of grace with confidence, that you may receive mercy and find grace in your time of need (Hebrews 4).

Splendid Savior,

It is my joy to trust and exalt You as the perfect source of eternal salvation to all who obey You.

Father, through Your Son I ask that I might never become dull of hearing, but instead crave solid food, developing skill in the word of righteousness. For solid food is for the mature. Therefore, please train my powers of discernment by constant practice to distinguish good from evil.

My soul, it is time to leave the elementary doctrine of Christ and go on to maturity, not laying again a foundation of repentance from dead works and of faith toward God. And this you will do if God permits.

Therefore, Father, please be willing! Please permit me to go on to maturity. Keep me, and may I never be one who is enlightened, tastes the heavenly gift, shares in the Holy Spirit, tastes of the goodness of Your word, and then falls away. May it never be! (Hebrews 5 & 6).

---

*I must secure more time for private devotions. I have been living far too public for me. The shortening of devotions starves the soul, it grows lean and faint. I have been keeping too late hours.* ~William Wilberforce

God of boundless mercy,

May I live as land that has drunk the rain that often falls on it, and produces a crop useful to those for whose sake it is cultivated, so that I might receive a blessing from You. But have mercy on me, lest I bear thorns and thistles, for such land is worthless and near to being cursed, and its end is to be burned.

Assure me of better things—things that belong to salvation. For You are not so unjust as to overlook my work and the love that I have shown for Your sake in serving the saints, as I still do. And I desire Your work in me, causing me to show the same earnestness to have the full assurance of hope until the end, so that I may not be sluggish, but an imitator of those who through faith and patience inherit the promises.

Convince me by the unchangeable character of Your purpose that I am an heir of the promise made to Abraham, that I might have strong encouragement to hold fast to the hope set before me.

O my soul, flee for refuge to Christ! For God has sworn by Himself and you have this promise as a sure and steadfast anchor of the soul, a hope that enters into the inner place behind the curtain, where Jesus has gone as a forerunner on our behalf, having become a high priest forever after the order of Melchizedek.

Lord Jesus, I exalt You as my hope and high priest! Please do not tarry in Your return (Hebrews 6).

O lofty Lover of broken men,

I come to You through Jesus, the guarantor of a better covenant. Instill within me the wondrous assurance that Christ holds His priesthood permanently, because He continues forever. Consequently, He is able to save to the uttermost those who draw near to You through Him, since He always lives to make intercession for them. May I entrust myself wholly to Him, for it is fitting that I should have such a high priest, holy, innocent, unstained, separated from sinners, and exalted above the heavens.

May I exalt Him, for He has no need, like other high priests, to offer sacrifices daily, first for His own sins and then for those of the people, since He did this once for all when he offered up Himself. For the law appoints men in their weakness as high priests, but the word of the oath, which came later than the law, appoints a Son who has been made perfect forever. Let me cling to Him all the more!

Lord Jesus, be praised and exalted in your holiness and perfection. Thank You that You always live to make intercession for me. Each day may I grow in love for Your appearing (Hebrews 7).

*There is not in the world a kind of life more sweet and delightful than that of a continual conversation with God.*
~Brother Lawrence

O God, my wealth and my salvation,

Sink deep within me the understanding that I have a perfect and powerful high priest, one who is seated at the right hand of the throne of the Majesty in heaven, a minister in the holy places in the true tent that You set up, not man. For Christ has obtained a ministry that is as much more excellent than the old as the covenant He mediates is better, since it is enacted on better promises. Cause me to trust Christ's sacrifice alone, who through the eternal Spirit offered Himself without blemish to You. By His blood purify my conscience from dead works to serve You.

Thank You that Christ, having been offered once to bear the sins of many, will appear a second time, not to deal with sin but to save those who are eagerly waiting for Him.

Father, grant me such eagerness, that I may look forward to the day when my glorified Savior returns. May I exult in His sacrifice, offered once for all time for sins, after which He sat down at Your right hand, waiting for that time until His enemies should be made a footstool for His feet. Oh let me praise and prize Him! For by a single offering He has perfected for all time those who are being sanctified (Hebrews 8, 9, 10).

*Prayer is as much a tool of our sanctification, by God's grace, as it is a tool of ministering God's grace to others.* ~Bruce Ware

Fearful Judge,

Since I now have confidence to enter the holy places by the blood of Jesus, by the new and living way that He opened for me through the curtain, that is, through His flesh, and since I have a great high priest over Your house, let me draw near to You with a true heart in full assurance of faith, with my heart sprinkled clean from an evil conscience and my body washed with pure water. May I hold fast the confession of my hope without wavering, for You who promised are faithful.

O my soul, let us consider how to stir one another to love and good works, not neglecting our time together, as is the habit of some, but encouraging one another, and all the more as we see the Day drawing near.

Father, keep me from going on sinning deliberately after receiving the knowledge of the truth, for if I do there no longer remains a sacrifice for sins, but a fearful expectation of judgment, and a fury of fire that will consume the adversaries. Please, please prevent me from spurning Your Son, or profaning the blood of the covenant by which I was sanctified, or outraging the Spirit of grace! For I know that vengeance is Yours; You will repay. "The Lord will judge His people." Sustain me! For it is a fearful thing to fall into the hands of the living God (Hebrews 10).

Self-sufficient God,

Only by Your worthy Son do I come to petition transforming and supporting grace. Because in You are all things good infinitely, I ask that You would grow me in kindness and sympathy. Make me a person who has compassion on those in prison, and who joyfully accepts the plundering of my property, knowing that I have a better possession and an abiding one. Let me not throw away my confidence, which has a great reward. For I have need of endurance, so that when I have done Your will I may receive what is promised. I thank You that I am not of those who shrink back and are destroyed, but of those who have faith and preserve their souls.

Raise me up as a person of faith, having the assurance of things hoped for, the conviction of things not seen. For without faith it is impossible to please You, for whoever would draw near to You must believe that You exist and that You reward those who seek You. Make me like Sarah, who by faith received power to conceive, even when she was past the age, since she considered You faithful to Your promise.

O my soul, even though men and women like Sarah were commended through their faith, they did not receive what was promised, since God had provided something better for us, that apart from us they should not be made perfect. And now we have the Lord Jesus Christ! Blessed be His name!

Father, we long to see Your matchless Son. Let us praise His name forever, to Your glory. Amen (Hebrews 10 & 11).

Disciplining Father,

Assist me to lay aside every weight, and sin which clings so closely, and let me run with endurance the race that is set before me, looking to Jesus, the founder and perfecter of my faith, who for the joy that was set before Him endured the cross, despising the shame, and is seated at the right hand of Your throne.

O my soul, consider Him who endured from sinners such hostility against Himself, so that you may not grow weary or fainthearted. In your struggle against sin you have not yet resisted to the point of shedding your blood.

Great Father, remind me of the exhortation that addresses me as a son: "My son, do not regard lightly the discipline of the Lord, nor be weary when reproved by Him. For the Lord disciplines the one He loves, and chastises every son whom He receives."

Assure me that it is for discipline that I have to endure—that You are treating me as a son. For if I am left without discipline, in which all have participated, then I am an illegitimate child and not a son. May I not begrudge Your correction, but respect You and be subject to You, understanding that You discipline me for my good, that I may share in Your holiness. When Your discipline seems painful rather than pleasant, make me confident that later it yields the peaceful fruit of righteousness to those who have been trained by it (Hebrews 12).

Gentle and fearful Healer,

I bow through the merit of my Lord Christ, asking that You would lift my drooping hands and strengthen my weak knees, and make straight paths for my feet, so that what is lame may not be put out of joint but rather be healed.

Cause me to strive for peace with everyone, and for the holiness without which no one will see You. May it never be that I fail to obtain Your grace! Protect me from any "root of bitterness" that springs up, causes trouble, and defiles many. Look after and guard my ways, that I may not be sexually immoral or unholy like Esau, who sold his birthright for a single meal. Have mercy! For I know that afterward, when he desired to inherit the blessing, he was rejected, for he found no chance to repent, though he sought it with tears.

O my soul, take refuge in Jesus, the mediator of a new covenant. See that you do not refuse the warnings of His Father. Flee to Christ, and you need not fear.

Father, help us as we strive to offer to You acceptable worship, with reverence and awe. For You are a consuming fire. Amen (Hebrews 12).

*Satan trembles when he sees*
*The weakest saint upon his knees.*
~William Cowper

Faithful Helper,

Under the supreme sacrifice of Your Son I come. Please form me into a person who does not neglect to show hospitality to strangers, for thereby some have entertained angels unawares. May I remember those who are in prison, as though in prison with them, and those who are mistreated.

Let marriage be held in honor by me, and help me to keep myself undefiled, for You will judge the sexually immoral and adulterous. Maintain my life free from the love of money, and make me content with what I have, for You have said, "I will never leave you nor forsake you."

Therefore, my soul, you can confidently say, "The Lord is my helper; I will not fear; what can man do to me?"

Father, remind me of my leaders, those who spoke to me Your word. May I consider the outcome of their way of life, and imitate their faith, for Jesus Christ is the same yesterday and today and forever. Guard me from being led away by diverse and strange teachings, for it is good for the heart to be strengthened by grace, not by the food of carnal wisdom, which has not benefited those devoted to it.

Please hasten the day of Your Son's appearing. Amen (Hebrews 13).

# My dazzling Delight,

Through Christ Jesus I ask that You would put a willingness in my heart to bear the reproach Your Son endured. May I grow to love the world less and love You more; to love myself less and love You more. For here I have no lasting city, but I seek the city that is to come. Through Christ then let me continually offer up a sacrifice of praise to You, that is, the fruit of lips that acknowledge His name. Let me not neglect to do good and to share what I have, for such sacrifices are pleasing to You.

Cause me to obey my leaders and submit to them, for they are keeping watch over my soul, as those who will have to give an account.

Now may You, the God of peace who brought again from the dead the Lord Jesus, the great shepherd of the sheep, by the blood of the eternal covenant, equip me with everything good that I may do Your will, working in me that which is pleasing in Your sight, through Jesus Christ, to whom be glory forever and ever. Amen (Hebrews 13).

*Power in prayer comes from being in touch with your weakness. To teach us how to pray, Jesus told stories of weak people who knew they couldn't do life on their own. The persistent widow and the friend at midnight get access, not because they are strong but because they are desperate. Learned desperation is at the heart of a praying life.*
~Paul Miller

My Sovereign Joy,

By Your beautiful Son and in His words I come before You. May I be counted among the poor in spirit, for theirs is the kingdom of heaven. Make me of those who mourn, for they shall be comforted. Bless me with meekness so that I will inherit the earth. Create within me a hunger and thirst for righteousness, so that I may be satisfied. Let me be merciful so that I may receive mercy. Give me a pure heart so that I might see You. Number me among the peacemakers, for they shall be called Your children. When I am persecuted for righteousness' sake, may I be heartened that I am blessed and that mine is the kingdom of heaven.

O my soul, let me remind you that you are blessed when others revile you and persecute you and utter all kinds of evil against you falsely on Christ's account. Rejoice and be glad, for your reward is great in heaven, for so they persecuted the prophets who were before you.

LORD, please be ever at work in me, molding me to be like Your Son. Amen (Matthew 5).

*To the degree you can shed the "unreality" of self-sufficiency, to that degree your prayer life will become richer and deeper.*
~Tim Keller

My gracious Father,

Through Jesus I kneel and ask that You would make me a brilliant light to the world. Let my light shine before others, so that they may see my good works and glorify You.

May I do Your commandments and teach them so that I will be called great in the kingdom of heaven. For unless my righteousness exceeds that of the scribes and Pharisees, I will never enter the kingdom of heaven. Keep me from becoming angry with my brother, from murdering him in my heart, and thus becoming liable to judgment. Keep me from looking with lustful intent, from committing adultery in my heart. If my right eye causes me to sin, let me tear it out and throw it away. For I would rather lose one of my members than have my whole body thrown into hell. Instill within me a healthy fear of eternal fire.

Grant me humble longsuffering so as not to resist the person who is evil. But if anyone slaps me on the right cheek, let me turn to him the other also. And if anyone would sue me and take my tunic, may I let him have my cloak as well. And if anyone forces me to go one mile, let me go with him two miles. Make me a person who gives to the one who begs from me, and who does not refuse the one who would borrow from me (Matthew 5).

Loving Shepherd,

Please listen to my prayer because of Your Son's righteousness. I ask that You would incline my heart to obey His commands. May I love my enemies and pray for those who persecute me, so that I may be Your child. For You make Your sun rise on the evil and the good, and send rain on the just and on the unjust.

O my soul, if you love those who love you, what reward do you have? Does not even the world do the same? You therefore must be perfect, as your heavenly Father is perfect.

Lord, by Your Spirit continually work Your perfection in me! Help me to abstain from practicing my righteousness before other people in order to be seen by them, for then I will have no reward from You.

When I give to the needy, do not let my left hand know what my right hand is doing, so that my giving may be in secret. For then You who see in secret will reward me.

And when I pray, keep me from being like the hypocrites who love to be seen and heard by others. Instead, cause me to go into my room and shut the door and pray to You who see in secret. Then, for what You see in secret please reward me. Amen (Matthew 5 & 6).

Faithful Father,

Through Your Son I ask that You would keep me obeying His words. May I not lay up for myself treasures on earth, where moth and rust destroy and where thieves break in and steal, but make me lay up for myself treasures in heaven, where neither moth nor rust destroys and where thieves do not break in and steal. For where my treasure is, there my heart will be also. And I long for my heart to love You unswervingly as its Treasure. I cannot serve two masters; I cannot serve You and money. Therefore keep me always as Your joyful, loyal servant.

Let me not be anxious about my life, what I will eat or what I will drink, nor about my body, what I will put on. For life is more than food, and the body more than clothing. Turn my eyes to the birds of the air and remind me—they neither sow nor reap nor gather into barns, and yet You feed them. And I am of much more value than they! Remind me that I cannot add a single hour to my span of life by being anxious. Guard me from being anxious about clothing, for the lilies of the field neither toil nor spin, yet even Solomon in all his glory was not arrayed like one of them.

My soul, trust your Master, lest He say, "O you of little faith." For if He clothes the grass of the field, which today is alive and tomorrow is thrown into the oven, will He not much more clothe you? Therefore do not be anxious, saying, "What shall we eat?" or "What shall we drink?" or "What shall we wear?" For everyone seeks after all these things, and your heavenly Father knows that you need them all. But seek first the kingdom of God and His righteousness, and all these things will be added to you.

Therefore, Father, may I not be anxious about tomorrow, for tomorrow will be anxious for itself. Sufficient for the day is its own trouble (Matthew 6).

---

*I would exhort those who have entertained a hope of their being true converts—and who since their supposed conversion have left off the duty of secret prayer, and ordinarily allow themselves in the omission of it—to throw away their hope. If you have left off calling upon God, it is time for you to leave off hoping and flattering yourselves with an imagination that you are the children of God. Probably it will be a very difficult thing for you to do this. It is hard for a man to let go a hope of heaven, on which he hath once allowed himself to lay hold, and which he hath retained for a considerable time. True conversion is a rare thing; but that men should be brought off from a false hope of conversion—after they are once settled and established in it, and have continued in it for some time—is much more rare.*
~Jonathan Edwards

Everlasting King,

I bow through Christ before You. May I judge not, that I be not judged. For with the judgment I pronounce I will be judged, and with the measure I use it will be measured to me. Guide me away from hypocrisy, to first take the log out of my own eye, so that then I will see clearly to take the speck out of my brother's eye.

Make me wise to avoid giving dogs what is holy, and to not throw my pearls before pigs, lest they trample them underfoot and turn to attack me.

Move me to ask, so that it will be given to me; to seek, so that I will find; to knock, so that it will be opened to me. Thank You for Your promise that everyone who asks receives, and the one who seeks finds, and to the one who knocks it will be opened. Remind me that if I, who am evil, know how to give good gifts to my children, how much more will my Father who is in heaven give good things to those who ask Him!

Whatever I wish that others would do to me, help me do also to them, for this is the Law and the Prophets. May I enter by the narrow gate. For the gate is wide and the way is easy that leads to destruction, and those who enter by it are many. For the gate is narrow and the way is hard that leads to life, and those who find it are few. Keep me steadfast on the hard way! May I never stray from it! For Your namesake let my foot not slip. Amen (Matthew 7).

Righteous Father,

Please protect me from false prophets, who come in sheep's clothing but inwardly are ravenous wolves. Make me wise to recognize them by their fruits. Help me to discern the healthy tree by its good fruit, and the diseased tree by its bad fruit. May I not be a diseased tree, for every such tree is cut down and thrown into the fire. Therefore, help me to bear much good fruit.

Let the warning of Your Son safeguard and preserve me when He says, "Not everyone who says to me, 'Lord, Lord,' will enter the kingdom of heaven, but the one who does the will of my Father who is in heaven." May He not say to me, "I never knew you; depart from me, you worker of lawlessness." Instead, please let me hear the words, "Well done, good and faithful servant." Through Jesus and by Your wonderful Spirit I ask these things. Amen (Matthew 7 & 25).

*The Spirit has much to do with acceptable prayer, and His work in prayer is too much neglected. He enlightens the mind to see its wants, softens the heart to feel them, quickens our desires after suitable supplies, gives clear views of God's power, wisdom, and grace to relieve us, and stirs up that confidence in His truth which excludes all wavering. Prayer is, therefore, a wonderful thing. In every acceptable prayer the whole Trinity is concerned. ~J. Angell James*

Revealer of Truth,

Through Christ I ask that You would make me hear His words and do them, so that I may be like a wise man who built his house on a rock. Keep me from merely hearing His words and not doing them, for then I will be like the foolish man who built his house on the sand. When the rain falls, and the floods come, and the winds blow and beat against me, I do not wish to fall! Your Word alone stands firm. May I build my life upon it.

Let me never despise or neglect tax collectors and sinners. But instead fill me with tenderness and comp-assion for them, and the humility to eat with them. For those who are well have no need of a physician, but those who are sick. Continue to teach me what this means: "I desire mercy, and not sacrifice." For Your great Son came not to call the righteous, but sinners (Matthew 7 & 9).

*The praying life is inseparable from obeying, loving, waiting, and suffering.* ~Paul Miller

My Supreme and Everlasting Joy,

In this world I am as a sheep in the midst of wolves, so please help me to be wise as a serpent and innocent as a dove. Prepare me for the persecution that lies along my pathway to heaven. Strengthen me to stand fast when men deliver me over to courts and flog me in their churches.

O my soul, when you are dragged before governors and kings for Christ's sake, do not be anxious how you are to speak or what you are to say, for what you are to say will be given to you in that hour. For it is not you who speak, but the Spirit of your Father speaking through you.

Lord God, make ready my heart for that dreadful time when brother will deliver brother over to death, and the father his child, and children will rise up against parents and have them put to death, and I will be hated by all for the sake of Christ's name. May I endure to the end and so be saved! Keep me! For Your hand is mightier than my own. Amen (Matthew 10).

*Prayer—secret, fervent, believing prayer—lies at the root of all personal godliness.* ~William Carey

Delectable God,

Grant me the grace to love Christ more than my father or mother, more than my son or daughter. For Your Son has said that if I fail to love Him supremely, I am not worthy of Him. And if I do not take my cross and follow Him, I am not worthy of Him. Therefore, because of Your grace and steadfast love, enable me to do so!

May I not find my life in this world and so lose it, but make me a person who gladly loses my life for Jesus' sake so that I might find it.

Father, I know that it pleases You well to hide things from the wise and understanding and reveal them to little children. Therefore please grow me in childlikeness, show me Your matchless Son, and may He choose to reveal You increasingly to me.

O my soul, you who labor and are heavy laden, go to Christ, and He will give you rest. Take His yoke upon you, and learn from Him, for He is gentle and lowly in heart, and you will find rest for your soul.

Lord Christ, I praise and thank You that Your yoke is easy, and Your burden is light! Amen (Matthew 10 & 11).

Great Covenant Keeper,

I cannot speak good if I am evil. For out of the abundance of the heart the mouth speaks. Therefore fill me with good treasure so that I might bring forth good. Make Christ my Treasure, so that I might speak His praise. For on the day of judgment I will give account for every careless word I speak; so please do not let me be condemned by my words.

I praise You that to me it has been given to know the secrets of the kingdom of heaven, for to many it has not been given. Let me never be among those of whom it is said, "Seeing they do not see, and hearing they do not hear, nor do they understand." Keep my heart from growing dull. Help me to see with my eyes and hear with my ears and understand with my heart and turn, that You may heal me.

O my soul, your master Jesus has said that blessed are your eyes, for they see, and your ears, for they hear. Truly, I say to you, many prophets and righteous people longed to see what you see, and did not see it, and to hear what you hear, and did not hear it.

Father, it is You who have opened my eyes to behold the wonders of Your word and the glories of Your Son. Keep me vigilant. Amen (Matthew 12 & 13).

*No man can do me a truer kindness in this world than to pray for me.* ~Charles Spurgeon

Self-exalting God,

May I never prove myself to be as one who, when I hear the word of the kingdom and do not understand it, the evil one comes and snatches away what has been sown in my heart. Guard me from the evil one! And let me not be like the one who hears the word and immediately receives it with joy, yet has no root in himself, but endures for a while, and when tribulation or persecution arises on account of the word, immediately falls away. Do not let me fall! Please grow my roots strong and deep in You.

Save me from being a person who hears the word, but the cares of the world and the deceitfulness of riches choke the word, and it proves unfruitful. Instead, make my heart good soil, so that I hear the word and understand it, and bear fruit and yield a hundredfold (Matthew 13).

*Prayer is continuing a conversation that God has started through his Word and his grace, which eventually becomes a full encounter with him.* ~Tim Keller

Sovereign Ruler and King,

Your Kingdom is like treasure hidden in a field, which a man found and covered up. Therefore, may I be like that man, who, in his joy went and sold all that he had and bought the field.

Again, make me like the merchant in search of fine pearls, who, on finding one pearl of great value, went and sold all that he had and bought it. Let me count Christ my greatest treasure, my most valuable pearl, my ultimate source of joy. And may I stop at nothing to have Him.

Keep me from breaking Your commandments for the sake of tradition. May I never, for the sake of tradition, make void Your word. Indeed, unless You preserve me with grace I will be numbered among the hypocrites who honor You with their lips, but their heart is far from You; who worship You in vain, teaching as doctrines the commandments of men.

Let me take heart, and not be afraid, for it is You who keep me. Let me not doubt, for truly Jesus, the Son of God, is my righteousness (Matthew 13, 14, 15).

*No praying man or woman accomplishes so much with so little expenditure of time as when he or she is praying.*
~A.E. McAdam

Lord of the heavens and the earth,

I come to You now petitioning more grace. My heart needs continual cleansing, because what proceeds from it is what defiles a person. For out of the heart come evil thoughts, murder, adultery, sexual immorality, theft, false witness, slander. These are what defile a person, therefore please create in me a clean heart.

O my soul, guard your heart. Watch and beware of the leaven of the Pharisees and Sadducees, of the sophistry of this age, of the false teachers who speak sweetly and humbly. Blessed are you if you know the truth of Christ. For flesh and blood has not revealed Him to you, but your Father who is in heaven.

O God, may I set my mind on the things of You, and not on the things of man. All this I ask in the name of the Christ, the Son of the living God. Amen (Matthew 15 & 16).

*Take Jesus at his word. Ask him. Tell him what you want. Get dirty. Write out your prayer requests; don't mindlessly drift through life on the American narcotic of busyness. If you try to seize the day, the day will eventually break you. Seize the corner of his garment and don't let go until he blesses you. He will reshape the day. ~Paul Miller*

My Mighty Fortress,

Thank You for giving me Your Son. Assist me to continue going after Him, to deny myself and take up my cross and follow Him. May I not strive to save my life and so lose it, but let me lose my life for Jesus' sake so that I might find it.

O my soul, what will it profit you if you gain the whole world and forfeit your life? Or what shall you give in return for your life? For the Son of man is going to come with His angels in the glory of His Father, and then He will repay you according to what you have done.

Therefore, Father, cause me to continually consider Christ as more precious than life itself. For indeed He is! Remind me that unless I turn and become like a child, I will never enter the kingdom of heaven. Help me to constantly humble myself like a child, for such who do so are greatest in the kingdom of heaven. Amen (Matthew 16 & 18).

*All hell is vanquished when the believer bows his knee in importunate supplication. Beloved brethren, let us pray. We cannot all argue, but we can all pray; we cannot all be leaders, but we can all be pleaders; we cannot all be mighty in rhetoric, but we can all be prevalent in prayer. I would sooner see you eloquent with God than with men. Prayer links us with the Eternal, the Omnipotent, the Infinite, and hence it is our chief resort. . . . Be sure that you are with God, and then you may be sure that God is with you. ~Charles Spurgeon*

Holy Lord,

Compared to the rest of the world I am astonishingly rich. And only with difficulty will a rich person enter the kingdom of heaven. Therefore, if I will be saved, You must do what is impossible with man—give me a heart that cherishes You more than money, possessions, or comfort. Help me! For it is easier for a camel to go through the eye of a needle than for a rich person to enter Your kingdom. Praise be to Your name that with You all things are possible—that I can be saved!

Grant me the grace to leave houses or brothers or sisters or father or mother or children or lands, for the sake of Christ's name, so that I might receive a hundredfold and inherit eternal life. Amen (Matthew 19).

*Prayer is so great that wherever you look in the Bible, it is there. Why? Everywhere God is, prayer is. Since God is everywhere and infinitely great, prayer must be all-pervasive in our lives. ~Tim Keller*

Soul-Satisfying God,

I desire true greatness. May I seek to be a servant and slave, even as the Son of Man came not to be served but to serve, and to give His life as a ransom for many.

Please keep me loving You with all my heart and with all my soul and with all my mind. For that is the great and first commandment. And continue stirring me to love my neighbor as myself.

O Father, even as You grant me grace to adore You more, protect me from becoming a person who preaches, but does not practice. May I never tie up heavy burdens, hard to bear, and lay them on people's shoulders, and then be unwilling to move them with my finger. Instead, enable me to humbly offer myself as their servant. Amen (Matthew 20 & 23).

*I have so much business I cannot get on without spending three hours daily in prayer.* ~Martin Luther

**R**ighteous Father,

There are so many pitfalls of hypocrisy that threaten to destroy me. You alone can guard my footsteps from straying from the narrow path. Let me never become one who does all his deeds to be seen by others, loving the place of honor at feasts and the admiration of churches and greetings in the marketplaces and being called wise by others.

O my soul, do not glory in your wisdom, for all you have is because of Jesus. For you have an instructor, the Christ. Whoever exalts himself will be humbled, and whoever humbles himself will be exalted.

Again, Father, may I never shut the kingdom of heaven in people's faces. Spare me from becoming a child of hell! Have mercy and save me from such woe (Matthew 23).

*"Prayer doesn't work" often means "you didn't do my will, in my way, in my time."* ~Paul Miller

O God who is beauty's fairest pleasure,

Protect me. I dwell in a deceitful world; guard my mind. Keep me safe from blind guides and blind fools. Save me from following those who tithe generously and have neglected the weightier matters of the law: justice and mercy and faithfulness. May I not neglect these things, lest I be like the blind guides who strain out a gnat and swallow a camel!

Shield me also from the snare of merely external righteousness, like those who clean the outside of the cup and plate, but inside they are full of greed and self-indulgence. Please make me clean inside, that my outside also may be clean. Again, preserve me from becoming like a whitewashed tomb, which outwardly appears beautiful, but within is full of dead people's bones and all uncleanness. Woe to me if You do not rescue me from being one who outwardly appears righteous to others, but within is full of hypocrisy and lawlessness (Matthew 23).

*Prayer is designed by God to display his fullness and our need. Prayer glorifies God because it puts us in the position of the thirsty and God in the position of the all-supplying fountain.*
~John Piper

Mighty Ruler,

Please, because of Christ, hear my prayer, and see that no one leads me astray. For many will come in Jesus' name, saying, "I am the Christ," and they will lead many astray. And when I hear of wars and rumors of wars, see that I am not alarmed.

O my soul, do not be surprised or afraid when kingdoms deliver you up to tribulation and put you death. For the Son has warned you that you will be hated by all nations for His name's sake.

O Father, when many then fall away and betray one another and hate one another, let me not be one of them! Protect me from the many false prophets that will arise and lead many astray. And when lawlessness increases, do not let my love grow cold. But help me to endure to the end and be saved, and proclaim the gospel of the kingdom throughout the whole world as a testimony to all nations. Amen (Matthew 24).

Winsome Lord,

May I be like one of the wise virgins, who took flasks of oil with their lamps. So that when the cry comes at midnight, "Here is the bridegroom! Come out to meet Him," I may be ready to rise and go with Him to the marriage feast. Please keep me from being like the foolish virgins who took no oil, and so came late to the marriage feast. And finding the door shut, they were not allowed to enter.

O my soul, watch therefore, for you know neither the day nor the hour.

Again, Father, make me like the servants who doubled that with which their master had entrusted them before he went on a long journey. May I deal wisely with what You have given me, so that when You return You will say, "Well done, good and faithful servant. You have been faithful over a little; I will set you over much. Enter into the joy of your master." Keep me from being like the worthless, wicked, slothful servant who was cast into the outer darkness where there will be weeping and gnashing of teeth. Please preserve me by grace and wisdom.

Come quickly, Bridegroom and Master! (Matthew 25).

---

*You cannot simply manipulate God by the power of being confident in what you ask. There are moral guidelines. This is what Jesus is saying with the condition, "If . . . my words abide in you, ask whatever you wish, and it will be done for you" (John 15:7). The words of Jesus shape the attitude and content of our prayers.* ~John Piper

O Lover of the sheep,

Only You can keep me for Jesus Christ when He comes in His glory and sits on His glorious throne. So I ask that You would preserve me as one of Your sheep, to whom the Son of Man will say on that day, "Come, you who are blessed by my Father, inherit the kingdom prepared for you from the foundation of the world."

May I be a person who feeds the hungry, gives drink to the thirsty, welcomes the stranger, clothes the naked, and visits the sick and imprisoned.

O my soul, truly, I say to you, as you do it to one of the least of these, you do it to Christ.

Father, it is my fervent desire that I be such a righteous person so that I might enter into eternal life. Thank You for the promise that, as I strive to enter by the narrow gate, Christ is with me always, to the end of the age.

Our great Savior and King, we long for Your return. Amen (Matthew 25 & 28).

---

*People are far too complicated; the world is far too evil; and my own heart is too off center to be able to love adequately without praying. I need Jesus.* ~Paul Miller

Lord and Husband,

When I stray from Your love, however wicked my waywardness proves to be, please draw me back! Even when I forget You, allure me, and bring me into the wilderness, and speak tenderly to me. Make the Valley of Trouble a door of hope for me. May I answer You as in the days of my youth, as at the time when I came out of the land of bondage. And let me call You "My Husband." Make me lie down in safety and remind me that You have betrothed me to Yourself forever.

O my soul, forsake not your Husband! For He has betrothed you to Himself in righteousness and in justice, in steadfast love and in mercy. He has betrothed you to Himself in faithfulness. And you have known Him!

Father, be pleased to guard me from abandoning faithfulness, steadfast love, and the knowledge of You. Save me from being destroyed for lack of knowledge, from forsaking You to cherish whoredom, wine, and new wine, which take away the understanding. Preserve me, for a people without understanding shall come to ruin (Hosea 2 & 4).

*Praying is the same to the new creature as crying is to the natural. The child is not learned by art or example to cry, but instructed by nature; it comes into the world crying. Praying is not a lesson got by forms and rules of art, but flowing from principles of new life itself.* ~William Gurnall

Redeeming Lover,

I thank You that, even when I played the whore and did not know You, and even as I stumbled in my guilt, You knew me, and my way was not hidden from You. Graciously You tore me that You might heal me; You struck me down, and You bound my wounds. Then You revived me and raised me up, that I might live before You. Praise be to You, LORD God! For You made me acknowledge my guilt and seek Your face. You caused me to turn to Yourself and to seek You earnestly in my distress.

O my soul, know; press on to know the LORD; His going out is sure as the dawn; He will come to you as the showers, as the spring rains that water the earth.

And now LORD God, let me not resemble Ephraim and Judah, whose love was like the morning cloud, like the dew that goes early away. Increase within me steadfast love for Your name. For You desire steadfast love and not sacrifice, the knowledge of God rather than burnt offerings. Prevent me from defiling myself with other lovers. And continue to restore me. Amen (Hosea 5, 6, 7).

*We look at the inadequacy of our praying and give up, thinking something is wrong with us. God looks at the adequacy of his Son and delights in our sloppy, meandering prayers.*
~Paul Miller

Most Holy Judge,

I am not immune to the subtle deceitfulness of sin. Therefore please protect me; increase my wisdom. Let me not be like a dove, silly and without sense. Woe to me if I stray from You! Only destruction will I find if You do not keep me.

May I never cry falsely, "My God, I—Your child—know You," when I have transgressed Your covenant and rebelled against Your law. Restrain me from making idols with my silver and gold. And forbid that I ever become incapable of innocence.

O my soul, cling to your righteous Husband! Fear the LORD and turn away from evil, lest you find yourself to be a useless vessel, and begin to regard His laws as a strange thing.

Father, may I not forget my Maker! Let me not grow to love a prostitute's wages. May I consecrate myself always to You and not to anything shameful, lest I become detestable like the thing I love. Preserve my glory and righteousness. Accept me because I listen to You, and make me bear much fruit in Your house. Show Your love to me, that my children may see many days (Hosea 7, 8, 9).

*Cold prayers always freeze before they reach heaven.*
~Thomas Brooks

Merciful Leader of wayward children,

Please continue growing me into a luxuriant vine that yields its fruit. But as my fruit increases, may I not use it to improve my pursuit of self or foreign altars. Guard my heart from becoming false, saying, "I have no king, for I do not fear the LORD." Such is the danger if You do not keep me. Unless You continue with me I will utter mere words; with empty oaths I will make covenants. Let me not be put to shame!

O my soul, He has kindly spared your neck. Do not make Him put you to the yoke to plow and harrow for yourself. Instead, sow for yourself righteousness; reap steadfast love.

LORD God, break up my fallow ground and let me seek You, that You may come and rain righteousness upon me.

Have mercy on me, for I have plowed iniquity; I have reaped injustice; I have eaten the fruit of lies. I have trusted in my own way; do not destroy me! Because of my great evil I appeal to the righteousness of Christ, for apart from Him I should be dashed in pieces and utterly cut off.

O great Son of David, I praise Your Name and bow with trembling, thankful heart. Hasten Your glorious return! Amen (Hosea 10).

**M**ost High Father,

Thank You that, when I was a child, You loved me, and out of Egypt You called me. Thank You for persisting, even when the more I was called, the more I went away and kept sacrificing to the gods of this world and burning offerings to self. Even so it was You who taught me to walk; You took me up by my arms, and now I know that You healed me. Let me rejoice and sing for joy. For You led me with cords of kindness, with the bands of love, and You became to me as one who eases the yoke on my jaws, and You bent down to me and fed me.

O my soul, take care, and keep your soul diligently, lest you forget the things that your eyes have seen, and lest they depart from your heart all the days of your life.

Sovereign LORD, when my heart is bent on turning away from You, may Your compassion grow warm and tender. On account of Christ Jesus do not execute Your burning anger; for You are God and not a man, the Holy One in our midst, and because of Your great mercy do not come in wrath.

If I stray, roar like a lion, so that when You roar I shall come trembling; I shall return trembling like a bird from Egypt. Then may I walk with You and remain faithful to the Holy One (Hosea 11 & Deuteronomy 4).

---

*I had rather learn what some men really judge about their own justification from their* prayers *than their writings.* ~John Owen

Lord God of hosts,

May I, by Your help, hold fast to love and justice, and wait continually for You. Keep me from incurring guilt and forsaking Christ. For if I do I shall be like the morning mist or like the dew that goes early away, like the chaff that swirls from the threshing floor or like smoke from a window. You are the Lord our God; we know no God but You, and besides You there is no savior. It was You who knew me in the wilderness, in the land of drought. But now, when I am filled, and my heart is lifted up, let me not forget You.

Even when I turn away from my Helper, because of Christ, do not destroy me. I thank You for His sacrifice on my behalf, so that You will not devour me and rip me open in Your wrath.

O my soul, bless the Name of Jesus, for He has ransomed you from the power of Sheol! He has redeemed you from Death. O Death, where are your plagues? O Sheol, where is your sting? The sting of death is sin, and the power of sin is the law. But thanks be to God, who gives us the victory through our Lord Jesus Christ.

Lord God, let not compassion be hidden from Your eyes toward me. May I flourish, and may my fountain never dry up. Amen (Hosea 12, 13, I Corinthians 15).

Lord God of Israel,

Continue in faithful mercy toward me. Turn Your anger from me and love me freely. Be like the dew to me, causing me to blossom like the lily, and take root like the trees of Lebanon. Then my shoots shall spread out; my beauty shall be like the olive, and my fragrance like Lebanon. Let me dwell beneath Your shadow; may I flourish like the grain and blossom like the vine; make my fame be like the wine of Lebanon.

O my soul, what has the Lord God to do with idols? It is He who answers and looks after you. He is like an evergreen cypress; from Him comes your fruit.

Sovereign Lord, let me be wise and understand these things; give me discernment to know them; for Your ways are right, and the upright walk in them, but transgressors stumble in them (Hosea 14).

*In God's commands to pray, we are compelled by the force of divine authority to come and drink of the living water, to receive bread from heaven, and to realize afresh moment by moment that all that we long for, and everything that is good, is found in one and only one place: in God.*
~Bruce Ware

Lord of Zion,

Thank You that through Christ I am washed; I am made clean; the evil of my deeds is removed from before Your eyes because He has borne my punishment. Assist me now to cease to do evil, learn to do good, seek justice, correct oppression, bring justice to the fatherless, plead the widow's cause.

Come now, my soul, let us reason together: though your sins were like scarlet, they are now white as snow; though they were red like crimson, they have now become like wool. Trust Christ for your righteousness! He is a great Savior.

Come, Lord God, and lead me up to Your mountain, to the house of the God of Jacob, that You may teach me Your ways and that I may walk in Your paths. O Lord, let me walk in Your light.

Let me stop regarding man in whose nostrils is breath, for of what account is he? Instead, give me more regard for Christ, so that on the day of the Lord I will not need to hide in the dust from before Your terror, and from the splendor of Your majesty. Prepare me for that day, when the haughty looks of man shall be brought low, and the lofty pride of men shall be humbled, and You alone will be exalted (Isaiah 1 & 2).

Eternal Source of all good,

Please continue to restrain the wicked inclinations that remain in my heart. For if You do not, I will soon become haughty and walk with an outstretched neck, glancing wantonly with my eyes. Go on with Your work of making me holy, washing away the filth of Your child, and cleansing my bloodstains by a spirit of purging.

Thank You for loving me as a choice vineyard, and planting me with choice vines on a fertile hill. Now let me yield grapes, and not wild grapes.

O my soul, you are the LORD's pleasant planting. Therefore, do not feast with tambourine and flute and wine, and disregard the deeds of the LORD, or turn a blind eye to the work of His hands.

LORD of hosts, let me never be found lacking in the knowledge of You, so that I may not condemn myself to exile, hunger, and thirst. For before You man is humbled, and each one is brought low, and the eyes of the haughty are brought low. But You are exalted in justice, and You show Yourself holy in righteousness (Isaiah 3, 4, 5).

*I have been benefited by praying for others; for by making an errand to God for them I have gotten something for myself.*
~Samuel Rutherford

Lord of hosts,

Guard me from those who draw iniquity with cords of falsehood, who draw sin as with cart ropes. Protect me from those who call evil good and good evil, who put darkness for light and light for darkness, who put bitter for sweet and sweet for bitter! There are many who are wise in their own eyes, and shrewd in their own sight; let me not be found among them. Make me stand firm and humble in the midst of those who are heroes at drinking wine, who acquit the guilty for a bribe, and deprive the innocent of his right. For they have rejected Your law, and have despised the word of the Holy One of Israel. Therefore, their root will be as rottenness, and their blossom will go up like dust.

O my soul, sing the words of the seraphim. "Holy, holy, holy is the Lord of hosts; the whole earth is full of His glory!" Behold, through Christ your guilt is taken away, and your sin atoned for. Therefore, you can now rejoice when your eyes see the King, the Lord of hosts.

Help me to remain firm in faith, O Lord. For if I am not firm in faith, I will not be firm at all. And let me not fear what the world fears, nor be in dread. But You, O Lord of hosts—may I regard You as holy. May You be my fear, and may You be my dread. Amen (Isaiah 5, 6, 7, 8).

O mniscient Father,

Thank You that I, who walked in darkness, have seen a great light; I used to dwell in a land of deep darkness, but now on me light has shined. Please multiply my fruit; increase my joy; may I rejoice before You as with joy at the harvest, as those who are glad when they divide great spoil. For the yoke of my burden, and the staff for my shoulder, and the rod of my oppressor, You have broken as on the day of Midian. For to us a child was born, to us the Son was given; and the government is upon His shoulder, and His name is called Wonderful Counselor, Mighty God, Everlasting Father, Prince of Peace.

O my soul, adore your great Savior! Of the increase of His government and of peace there will be no end. He has established it and upholds it with justice and with righteousness from this time forth and forevermore.

O LORD of hosts, thank You that Your zeal has accomplished salvation for me through Christ. Amen (Isaiah 9).

---

*In personal relationships, if we attempt to fake emotional intensity and put on an outward show of emotion that is not consistent with the feelings of our hearts, others involved will usually sense our hypocrisy at once and be put off by it. How much more is this true of God, who fully knows our hearts. Therefore, intensity and depth of emotional involvement in prayer should never be faked: we cannot fool God.* ~Wayne Grudem

Majestic One,

In this day let me lean on You, the Holy One of Israel, in truth. Please continue to change me into the likeness of the shoot that came forth from the stump of Jesse. May Your Spirit rest upon me, the Spirit of wisdom and understanding, the Spirit of counsel and might, the Spirit of knowledge and the fear of the LORD. And let my delight be always in the fear of You. Clothe me with righteousness as the belt of my waist, and faithfulness as the belt of my loins.

I will give thanks to You, O LORD, for though You were once angry with me, Your anger turned away because of Christ, that You might comfort me.

O my soul, God is your salvation; trust, and do not be afraid; for the LORD GOD is your strength and your song, and He has become your salvation!

Therefore, O God, cause me to draw water from the wells of salvation with joy. And may I give thanks to You, call upon Your name, make known Your deeds among the peoples, and proclaim that Your name is exalted. May I sing praises to You, for You have done gloriously; let me make this known in all the earth. Let us shout together and sing for joy, for great in our midst are You, O Holy One of Israel (Isaiah 10, 11, 12).

Sovereign, eternal, unchangeable LORD,

You are my God; I will exalt You; I will praise Your name, for You have done wonderful things, plans formed of old, faithful and sure. You have made me; I am the work of Your hands. Let me glorify You; let me fear You. May You be to me a stronghold; a stronghold when I am needy and in distress, my shelter from the storm and my shade from the heat.

May I hope and long for the day when You will make for all peoples a feast of rich food, a feast of well-aged wine, of rich food full of marrow, of aged wine well refined.

O my soul, on that day He will swallow up death forever; and the Lord GOD will wipe away tears from all faces, and the reproach of His people He will take away from all the earth, for the LORD has spoken.

You are my God; I have waited for You, that You might save me. You are the LORD; I have waited for You; let me be glad and rejoice in Your salvation. Keep me in perfect peace because my mind is stayed on You, because I trust in You. Help me to trust in You forever, for You are an everlasting rock (Isaiah 25 & 26).

*You should, in Tertullian's phrase, with a holy conspiracy, besiege heaven.* ~Thomas Manton

O LORD my God,

Please make level my path; for You make the way of the righteous level. In the path of Your judgments, O LORD, let me wait for You; may Your name and remembrance be the desire of my soul. Make my soul yearn for You in the night; cause my spirit within me to earnestly seek You. For when Your judgments are in the earth, the inhabitants of the world learn righteousness.

O LORD, ordain peace for me; do for me all my works. Even though other lords besides You may rule over me, let me bring Your name alone to remembrance.

Let me trust You, for You, the LORD, are my keeper; every moment You water me as a vineyard. You keep me night and day; may I lay hold of Your protection. In the days to come let me blossom and put forth shoots and fill the whole world with fruit. Amen (Isaiah 26 & 27).

---

*Prayer is the way that all the things we believe in and that Christ has won for us actually become our strength. Prayer is the way that truth is worked into your heart to create new instincts, reflexes, and dispositions.* ~Tim Keller

Lord of power,

Please be to me a crown of glory and a diadem of beauty. For You are the Lord of hosts, wonderful in counsel and excellent in wisdom.

Protect me from hypocrisy. May it never be that I draw near with my mouth and honor You with my lips, while my heart is far from You. Let my fear of You be genuine, and not a commandment taught by men.

O my soul, guard your heart, lest you turn things upside down and regard the Potter as the clay.

O Lord, keep me from saying of my Maker, "He did not make me"; or of You who formed me, "He has no understanding." Instead, let me be turned into a fruitful field. Out of my gloom and darkness cause me to see and obtain fresh joy in You. May I exult in You, the Holy One of Israel, and no more be ashamed. Let me see the work of Your hands and sanctify Your name; let me sanctify the Holy One of Jacob and stand in awe of the God of Israel (Isaiah 28 & 29).

*Just as God's Word must reform our theology, our ethics, and our practices, so also must it reform our praying.* ~D.A. Carson

Exalted Fountain of Grace,

May I find my strength in quietness and in trust, for You wait to be gracious to me. Therefore, exalt Yourself to show mercy to me. For You are a God of justice; blessed are all those who wait for You. Gather me into Your arms so that I will weep no more.

O my soul, He will surely be gracious to you at the sound of your cry. As soon as He hears it, He answers you.

Let me trust Your promise, O LORD, that though You give me the bread of adversity and the water of affliction, yet You will not hide Yourself forever, but my eyes shall see my Teacher. And may my ears hear a word behind me, saying, "This is the way, walk in it," when I turn to the right or when I turn to the left. Let me also defile my idols of the flesh, and scatter them as unclean things, saying to them, "Be gone!"

Cause my hope to remain rooted and steadfast in You when calamity overtakes me. For soon the light of the moon will be as the light of the sun, and the light of the sun will be sevenfold, as the light of seven days, in the day when You bind up the brokenness of Your people, and heal the wounds inflicted by Your blow. With Your burning anger devour my enemies, and give me a song as in the night when a holy feast is kept, and gladness of heart, as when one sets out to the sound of the flute to go to the mountain of the LORD, to the Rock of Israel. Cause Your majestic voice to be heard by me. Amen (Isaiah 30).

Worker of wonders,

Continue to make me righteous, so that I may have peace, quietness, and security forever. O LORD, be gracious to me; I wait for You. Be my arm every morning, my salvation in the time of trouble. For You are exalted, for You dwell on high; fill me with justice and righteousness, and be the stability of my days, abundance of salvation, wisdom, and knowledge; let the fear of You be my treasure. Arise, O LORD, lift Yourself up; be exalted in me.

Help me to become a person who walks righteously and speaks uprightly, who despises the gain of oppressions, who shakes my hands, lest they hold a bribe, who stops my ears from hearing of bloodshed and shuts my eyes from looking on evil. Then I will dwell on the heights; my place of defense will be the fortress of rocks; my bread will be given me; my water will be sure.

Let my eyes behold You in Your beauty. Be with me in majesty, for You are my judge; You are my lawgiver; You are my king; You will save me (Isaiah 32 & 33).

Beautiful LORD,

Let me be glad as I look to the day of the Son's return. May I rejoice and blossom like the crocus; let me blossom abundantly and rejoice with joy and singing. And may I long to see Your glory, the majesty of my God. Strengthen my weak hands, and make firm my feeble knees.

O my soul, be not anxious of heart. Be strong; fear not! Behold, your God will come with vengeance, with the recompense of God. He will come and save you. Then the eyes of the blind shall be opened, and the ears of the deaf unstopped; then shall the lame man leap like a deer, and the tongue of the mute sing for joy.

Prepare me, O LORD, to set foot on the great highway, which shall be called the Way of Holiness; for the unclean shall not pass over it. It shall belong to those who walk on the way; let me not go astray. Let me yearn for that day when the redeemed shall walk there, when the ransomed of the LORD shall return and come to Zion with singing. Everlasting joy shall be upon their heads; they shall obtain gladness and joy, and sorrow and sighing shall flee away (Isaiah 35).

*God can pick sense out of a confused prayer.* ~Richard Sibbes

O LORD of hosts, God of Israel,

Enthroned above the cherubim, You are the God, You alone, of all the kingdoms of the earth; You have made heaven and earth; You have made me. Incline Your ear, O LORD, and hear; open Your eyes, O LORD, and see; and hear all the words of those who mock You, the living God. Truly, O LORD, there are many who desire to lay waste all the fruit of my hands. In their wickedness they have destroyed others and cast their gods into the fire—the work of men's hands, wood and stone. So now, O LORD my God, save me from their hands, that all the kingdoms of the earth may know that You alone are the LORD. Please defend me to save me, for Your own sake.

Please, O LORD, remember me and cause me to walk before You in faithfulness and with a whole heart, and to do what is good in Your sight. May I trust that it is for my welfare when I have great bitterness; let me praise You and hope for Your faithfulness.

O my soul, in love He has delivered your life from the pit of destruction, for He has cast all your sins behind His back.

Let me thank You, O LORD, as I do this day; let me make known to my children Your faithfulness. For it is You who will save us, and we will play music on stringed instruments all the days of our lives, at the house of the LORD (Isaiah 37 & 38).

# Wonderful God,

Thank You that you comfort me. Thank You for speaking tenderly to me and crying to me that my iniquity is pardoned, that because of Christ I have not received from Your hand double for all my sins. May I wait patiently for the day when Your glory shall be revealed, and all flesh shall see it together, for You have spoken.

O my soul, all flesh is grass, and all its beauty is like the flower of the field. The grass withers, the flower fades when the breath of the LORD blows on it; surely the people are grass. The grass withers, the flower fades, but the word of God will stand forever.

Lord GOD, let me behold You coming with might; with Your arm ruling for You. Please tend me like a shepherd; gather me into Your arms; carry me in Your bosom, and gently lead me.

May I worship You as the only one who has measured the waters in the hollow of his hand and marked off the heavens with a span, enclosed the dust of the earth in a measure and weighed the mountains in scales and the hills in a balance. I praise You, for no man has directed Your Spirit or shown You his counsel. Amen (Isaiah 40).

---

*As highly as Paul values marital obligations, he can envisage a couple self-consciously choosing not to have sex together for a while, so that the time they would have spent pleasing each other sexually will be devoted to prayer. That says something about Paul's valuation of prayer.* ~D. A. Carson

Creator of the ends of the earth,

Be exalted in Your wisdom and fullness, for You have never needed anyone. Whom did You consult, and who made You understand? Who taught You the path of justice, and taught You knowledge, and showed You the way of understanding? Behold, the nations are like a drop from a bucket, and are accounted as the dust on the scales; behold, You take up the coastlands like fine dust. Lebanon would not suffice for fuel, nor are its beasts enough for a burnt offering. All the nations are as nothing before You, they are accounted by You as less than nothing and emptiness.

Therefore, I worship and adore Your greatness, taking comfort that You are powerful and lack nothing.

O my soul, to whom then will you liken God, or what likeness compare with Him? You have known and heard, and it has been told you from the beginning, that it is He who sits above the circle of the earth, and its inhabitants are like grasshoppers; who stretches out the heavens like a curtain, and spreads them like a tent to dwell in; who brings princes to nothing, and makes the rulers of the earth as emptiness.

O Holy One, to whom then will I compare You, that You should be like him? Lift up my eyes on high to see: You created the stars—You who bring out their host by number, calling them all by name, by the greatness of Your might, and because You are strong in power not one is missing (Isaiah 40).

Y ou who alone are the true God,

May I never complain that my way is hidden from You, or that my right is disregarded by my God. Instead, assure me that You are the everlasting God, the Creator of the ends of the earth. Instill within me a steadfast confidence in You, for You do not faint or grow weary; Your understanding is unsearchable. Give power to me when I am faint, and when I have no might increase my strength. Even when I faint and become weary, when I fall exhausted, let me wait on You. For they who wait for You shall renew their strength; they shall mount up with wings like eagles; they shall run and not be weary; they shall walk and not faint.

Thank You for choosing me, for taking me from the pit, for calling me out of bondage, saying to me, "You are my servant, I have chosen you and not cast you off."

O my soul, fear not, for He is with you; be not dismayed, for He is your God; He will strengthen, He will help you, He will uphold you with His righteous right hand.

O LORD my God, hold my right hand, and say to me, "Fear not, I am the one who helps you" (Isaiah 40 & 41).

*Intercession is more than specific: it is pondered: it requires us to bear on our heart the burden of those for whom we pray.*
~George A. Buttrick

King of Jacob,

Defend me from all who are incensed against me; let them be put to shame and confounded; may those who strive against me be as nothing and perish. Let the evil ones who war against me be as nothing at all.

Fear not, my soul! He is the one who helps you; your Redeemer is the Holy One of Israel.

O LORD, let me rejoice in You; in the Holy One of Israel let me glory. When I am poor and needy and seek for water, and there is none, and my tongue is parched with thirst, please answer me; O God of Israel, do not forsake me. Open rivers on the bare heights, and fountains in the midst of the valleys. Make the wilderness a pool of water, and the dry land springs of water for me. Put in my wilderness the cedar, the acacia, the myrtle, and the olive. Set in my desert the cypress, the plane and the pine together, that I may see and know, may consider and understand, that Your hand has done it, the Holy One of Israel has created it.

Increase my soul's delight in Your Servant, whom You uphold, Your chosen, just as Your soul delights in Him. May I hope in Him, for a bruised reed He will not break, and a faintly burning wick He will not quench; He will faithfully bring forth justice. Hasten the day of His return! Amen (Isaiah 41 & 42).

O God, the LORD,

Who created the heavens and stretched them out, who spread out the earth and what comes from it, who gives breath to the people on it and spirit to those who walk in it, reassure me that You are the LORD, and have called me in righteousness. Take me by the hand and keep me. Conform me into the image of Him who is given as a covenant for the people, a light for the nations, to open the eyes that are blind, to bring out the prisoners from the dungeon, from the prison those who sit in darkness.

O my soul, pursue Christ! Esteem Christ! Honor His Father, for He is the LORD; that is His name; His glory He gives to no other, nor His praise to carved idols.

Let me sing to You a new song, O LORD, Your praise from the end of the earth. Let me lift up my voice along with the sea, and all that fills it, the coastlands and their inhabitants, the desert and its cities. May I sing for joy, and shout from the top of the mountains. Let me give glory to You, and declare Your praise in the coastlands. For You go out like a mighty man, like a man of war You stir up Your zeal; You cry out, You shout aloud, You show Yourself mighty against Your foes.

Lead me in a way that I do not know, in paths that I have not known please guide me. Turn the darkness before me into light, the rough places into level ground. For these are the things that You do, and You will not forsake me (Isaiah 42).

H oly LORD,

Be pleased, for Your righteousness' sake, to magnify Your law and make it glorious through me. Be exalted, for You created me, You formed me. May I fear not, for You have redeemed me; You have called me by name, I am Yours. When I pass through the waters, please be with me; and through the rivers, let them not overwhelm me; when I walk through fire let me not be burned, and may the flame not consume me. For You are the LORD my God, the Holy One of Israel, my Savior.

O my soul, because you are precious in His eyes, and honored, and He loves you, He gives men in return for you, peoples in exchange for your life. Fear not, for He is with you. He is the LORD, and besides Him there is no savior.

Let me adore You as the LORD, my Redeemer, my Holy One, the Creator of Israel, my King. Give water to me in the wilderness, rivers when I am in the desert, to give drink to Your chosen one, the person whom You formed for Yourself that I might declare Your praise. Thank You that You are He who blots out my transgressions for Your own sake, and You will not remember my sins. For I am Your servant whom You have chosen; You made me and formed me from the womb. Help me, and let me not fear. Pour Your Spirit upon my offspring, and Your blessing on my descendants. Let them spring up among the grass like willows by flowing streams. May one say, "I am the LORD's," and another write on his hand, "The LORD's," and name himself by the name of Israel (Isaiah 42, 43, 44).

King and Redeemer of Israel,

Glory be to Your name, for You are the first and You are the last; besides You there is no god. Who is like You? Therefore, let me not fear, nor be afraid; for You declare what is to come, and what will happen. May I trust in You, for there is no god besides You, there is no Rock; I know not any.

Let me remember that all who fashion idols are nothing, and the things they delight in do not profit, for I am Your servant; You formed me; I am Your servant; let me not be forgotten by You.

O my soul, He has blotted out your transgressions like a cloud and your sins like mist; cling to Him, for He has redeemed you!

Sing, O heavens, for the LORD has done it; shout, O depths of the earth; break forth into singing, O mountains, O forest, and every tree in it! For You, LORD, have redeemed me, and will be glorified in me. Through me be pleased to display Your beauty. May I take comfort and rejoice in the knowledge that You formed me in the womb, that You are the LORD, who made all things, who alone stretched out the heavens, who spread out the earth by Yourself, who frustrates the signs of liars and makes fools of diviners, who turns wise men back and makes their knowledge foolish, who says to the deep, "Be dry; I will dry up your rivers." Let me love and fear You. Amen (Isaiah 44).

*All progress in prayer is an answer to prayer—our own or another's. And all true prayer promotes its own progress and increases our power to pray.* ~P.T. Forsyth

**L**ORD God of Israel, who calls His people by name,

I come before You because You are the LORD, and there is no other, besides You there is no God. Please equip me to make known Your might, that people may know, from the rising of the sun and from the west, that there is none besides You; You are the LORD, and there is no other. May I tremble and rejoice at the truth that You form light and create darkness. Let me worship and bow down before You as the one who makes well-being and creates calamity. May I exalt You as the LORD who does all these things.

O my soul, praise and adore Him with me! For He made the earth and created man on it; it was His hands that stretched out the heavens, and He commanded all their host.

Stir me up, O LORD, in righteousness, and make all my ways level. May the wealthy and men of stature come to me, saying, "Surely God is in you, and there is no other, no god besides Him."

Many make idols and go in confusion together. But I thank You that I am saved by You with everlasting salvation; I shall not be put to shame or confounded to all eternity. For You are the LORD and there is no other. You did not say to me, "Seek me in vain." You speak truth; You declare what is right (Isaiah 45).

*We don't need self-discipline to pray continuously; we just need to be poor in spirit.* ~Paul Miller

O God who hears prayer,

Let me turn continually to You for my salvation. For You are God, and there is no other. Therefore let me say of You, "Only in the LORD are righteousness and strength." Thank You that in You I am justified and can glory. Praise be to Your name, for I have been borne by You from before my birth, carried from the womb; even to my old age You are He, and to gray hairs You will carry me. You have made, and You will bear; You will carry and will save.

O my soul, remember with me that He is God, and there is no other; He is God, and there is none like Him, declaring the end from the beginning and from ancient times things not yet done, saying, "My counsel shall stand, and I will accomplish all my purpose."

Therefore, great LORD, may I trust the word that goes out from Your mouth in righteousness. Let me hope in You as the God who brings to pass what He speaks; who does what He has purposed. For Your name's sake be gracious to me, for the sake of Your praise make me walk in holiness, and do not cut me off. Refine me, and give me strength as You try me in the furnace of affliction. For Your own sake, for Your own sake, do this, for how should Your name be profaned? Your glory You will not give to another. Therefore magnify Yourself in me! Glorify Yourself through me! Use me to exalt the greatness of Your name. Amen (Isaiah 45, 46, 48).

**M**y Redeemer,

Teach me to profit from uprightness, and lead me in the way I should go. Make me pay attention to Your commandments so that my peace will be like a river, and my righteousness like the waves of the sea; then let my offspring be like the sand, and my descendents like its grains; may their name never be cut off or destroyed from before You.

Now, even now I shout for joy, for You have redeemed me! Therefore do not let me thirst when You lead me through deserts; make water flow for me even from the rocks, so that my soul is satisfied.

Make my mouth like a sharp sword; in the shadow of Your hand please hide me; make me a polished arrow; in Your quiver hide me away.

O my soul, you are the LORD's servant, in whom He will be glorified and display His beauty. You have not labored in vain; you have not spent your strength for nothing. For surely your recompense is with your God.

I will praise You, O LORD, for You called me from the womb, from the body of my mother You named my name. You formed me from the womb to be Your servant, therefore may I be honored in Your eyes, and may You continually be my strength. Make me as a light for the nations, that Your salvation may reach to the ends of the earth. Let kings see and arise; may princes prostrate themselves; because of You, who are faithful, the Holy One of Israel, who has chosen me (Isaiah 48 & 49).

Ruler of heaven and earth,

Please keep me. Answer me and help me; let me not hunger or thirst, and may neither scorching wind nor sun strike me. Have pity on me and lead me, and by springs of water guide me.

Sing for joy, O heavens, and exult, O earth; break forth, O mountains, into singing! For the LORD has comforted me and will have compassion on my affliction.

I praise You that You have not forsaken me; You have not forgotten me. Even a mother may forget her nursing child, yet You will not forget me. Assure me of this, and let me know that You are the LORD; those who wait for You shall not be put to shame. Fight for me; contend with those who contend with me. Then all flesh shall know that You are the LORD my Savior, and my Redeemer, the Mighty One of Jacob (Isaiah 49).

*The artless child is still the divine model for all of us. Prayer will increase in power and reality as we repudiate all pretense and learn to be utterly honest before God as well as before men.*
~A. W. Tozer

Forgiving God,

Thank You that Your hand is not shortened, that it can redeem me. For by Your power and rebuke You dry up the sea, and make the rivers a desert.

Please give me the tongue of those who are taught, that I may know how to sustain with a word those who are weary. Morning by morning awaken me; awaken my ear to hear as those who are taught.

When I am struck and spit upon for Your namesake fill me with hope in You, the Lord GOD. For You will help me; therefore I will not be disgraced. Remind me that I will not be put to shame, for You who vindicate me are near.

Let me fear You and obey the voice of Your servant, Christ. And when I walk in darkness and have no light let me trust in Your name and rely on you, my God. Cause me to pursue righteousness and seek You. Make my wilderness like Eden, my desert like the garden of the LORD; may joy and gladness be found in me, thanksgiving and the voice of song (Isaiah 50 & 51).

---

*Prayer is often represented as the great means of the Christian life. But it is no mere means, it is the great end of that life. It is, of course, not untrue to call it a means. It is so, especially at first. But at last it is truer to say that we live the Christian life in order to pray than that we pray in order to live the Christian life.* ~P.T. Forsyth

Lovely God,

Turn my attention to Yourself. Let me give ear to the law that has gone out from You, to the justice that You have set for a light to the peoples. May Your righteousness draw near to me, let Your salvation go out to me; make me hope for You, and for Your arm let me wait. Lift up my eyes to the heavens, and cause me to look at the earth beneath and see that the heavens will vanish like smoke, the earth will wear out like a garment, and they who dwell in it will die in like manner. But remind me that Your salvation will be forever, and Your righteousness will never be dismayed.

Listen to Him, O my soul, you who know righteousness; for He says, "Fear not the reproach of man, nor be dismayed at their revilings. For the moth will eat them up like a garment, and the worm will eat them like wool; but my righteousness will be forever, and my salvation to all generations."

Awake, awake, put on strength, O arm of the LORD; awake, as in days of old, the generations of long ago, and defend me. You have ransomed me, therefore let me come into Your presence with singing; crown my head with everlasting joy; grant me gladness and joy, so that sorrow and sighing shall flee away.

Teach me not to be afraid of man who dies, of the son of man who is made like grass, for You, You are He who comforts me. Let me take confidence in You, my Maker, who stretched out the heavens and laid the foundations of the earth, and may I fear not the oppressors who set themselves up to destroy (Isaiah 51).

Lord of the oceans,

Who stirs up the sea so that its waves roar, please put Your words in my mouth and cover me in the shadow of Your hand. For You are the LORD of hosts, who established the heavens and laid the foundations of the earth, and say to me, "You are my child."

Thank You for awakening me from the slumber of death, for clothing me with strength and beautiful garments. For I was sold for nothing, and You have redeemed me without money. Therefore make my feet beautiful upon the mountains, as one who brings good news, who publishes peace, who brings good news of happiness, who publishes salvation, who says, "My God reigns." Let me lift up my voice with my brothers and sisters, so that together we may sing for joy, and eye to eye await the return of Your Son.

O my soul, break forth into singing, for the LORD has comforted His people; He has redeemed even you! The LORD has bared His holy arm before the eyes of all the nations, and all the ends of the earth shall see the salvation of our God.

LORD, please go always before me; O God of Israel, be my rear guard. Amen (Isaiah 51 & 52).

---

*When our awareness of the greatness of God and the gospel is dim, our prayer lives will be small. The less we think of the nature and character of God, and the less we are reminded of what Jesus did for us on the Cross, the less we want to pray.*
*~Donald S. Whitney*

My Father and my God,

Grow within my heart a deep esteem for Him who has borne my griefs and carried my sorrows, who was wounded for my transgressions and crushed for my iniquities. May I treasure Him increasingly, desire Him more fervently, for upon Him was the chastisement that brought me peace, and with His stripes I am healed.

Let me love and cherish Him as the One stricken for my transgression. May I praise You with trembling for crushing Him so that I could be accounted righteous. Stir up gratitude within me for His sacrifice, for bearing my iniquities, pouring out His soul to death, and for making intercession for me.

Sing, O my soul! Break forth into singing and cry aloud! For you have been reconciled to your Maker and Husband, to the LORD of hosts; the Holy One of Israel is your Redeemer!

O LORD, thank You for calling me when I was like one deserted and grieved in spirit. And now be exalted for Your great compassion toward me! Keep me in Your sovereign arms. Amen (Isaiah 53 & 54).

God of the whole earth,

Do not hide Your beautiful face from me or be angry with me, but with everlasting love have compassion on me. Even though the mountains may depart and the hills be removed, let not Your steadfast love depart from me, and do not remove Your covenant of peace, but continue to have compassion on me.

O my soul, although you may be afflicted and storm-tossed, take comfort in His word! For behold, He will set your stones in antimony, and lay your foundations with sapphires. He will wall you in with precious stones.

LORD, please bless me, and may all my children be taught by You, and let the peace of my children be great. Establish me in righteousness; keep me far from oppression and fear. Protect me from terror; may it not come near me. I commit myself to Your hand, for You guard me so that no weapon that is fashioned against me shall succeed (Isaiah 54).

*Meditation is a middle sort of duty between the word and prayer, and hath respect to both. The word feedeth meditation, and meditation feedeth prayer. These duties must always go hand in hand; meditation must follow hearing and precede prayer. To hear and not to meditate is unfruitful. We may hear and hear, but it is like putting a thing into a bag with holes.... It is rashness to pray and not to meditate. What we take in by the word we digest by meditation and let out by prayer. These three duties must be ordered that one may not jostle out the other. Men are barren, dry, and sapless in their prayers for want of exercising themselves in holy thoughts.* ~Thomas Manton

Compassionate LORD,

When I thirst, draw me to the waters, draw me to Yourself. Keep me from spending my money for that which is not bread, and my labor for that which does not satisfy. Instead, make me listen diligently to You, and eat what is good, and delight myself in rich food—wine and milk without price. Incline my ear, and let me come to You; may I hear, that my soul may live, because of Your everlasting covenant of steadfast, sure love.

O my soul, seek the LORD while He may be found; call upon Him while He is near! Let us forsake our wicked ways and our unrighteous thoughts; and let us turn to the LORD, that He may have compassion on us, and to our God, for He will abundantly pardon.

Holy One of Israel, I bow before You, for Your thoughts are not my thoughts, neither are Your ways my ways. I worship and exalt You, for as the heavens are higher than the earth, so are Your ways higher than my ways and Your thoughts than my thoughts. Amen (Isaiah 55).

You who are high and lifted up,

Be pleased to fill me with joy and lead me forth in peace. May I keep justice, and do righteousness, for Your salvation has come, and Your deliverance is revealed. Keep my hand from doing any evil, and make me hold on to righteousness.

Thank You for saving me; for giving me an everlasting name that shall not be cut off. Let the mountains and the hills break forth into singing, and all the trees of the field clap their hands! For You have made a name for Yourself; You have redeemed me! Make me joyful in Your house of prayer.

Please protect me from blind watchmen without knowledge, from shepherds who have no understanding. Revive my spirit when I am lowly, and revive my heart when I am contrite. May I seek You daily and delight to know Your ways; let me delight to draw near to You. And when I fast, may it not be merely to quarrel and pursue my own business. But cause me to fast as You choose: to loose the bonds of wickedness, to undo the straps of the yoke, to let the oppressed go free, to share my bread with the hungry, to bring the homeless poor into my house, and to clothe the naked. Then may my light break forth like the dawn, and make righteousness go before me, with Your glory as my rear guard (Isaiah 55, 56, 58).

*A chief object of all prayer is to bring us to God....*
*The chief failure of prayer is its cessation.* ~P.T. Forsyth

You who inhabit eternity,

When I call to You, please answer. I cry out to you: keep me from speaking wickedness. But rather, may I pour myself out for the hungry and satisfy the desire of the afflicted, for then shall my light rise in the darkness and my gloom be as the noonday. Guide me continually and satisfy my desire in scorched places and make my bones strong; may I be like a watered garden, like a spring of water, whose waters do not fail. Let me take delight in You; feed me with the heritage of Jacob.

O my soul, arise, shine, for your light has come, and the glory of the LORD has risen upon you. Although darkness once covered you, now the LORD has risen upon you, and His glory is seen upon you. And nations shall come to your light, and kings to the brightness of Christ in you!

LORD God, may peoples see me and be radiant; let their hearts thrill and exult because of the abundance of my joy in Christ. Make me declare the good news—the praises of Christ. Beautify your servant so that the coastlands will hope for You, for the name of the LORD my God, and for the Holy One of Israel, because You have made me beautiful (Isaiah 58 & 60).

O God whose name is Holy,

In Your favor be pleased to have mercy on me. Make me majestic forever, and a joy to every age, so that all may know that You, the LORD, are my Savior and my Redeemer, the Mighty One of Jacob. Make my overseers peace and my taskmasters righteousness. May my clothing be called Salvation, and the gates to my house Praise.

O my soul, trust in the LORD, and He will be your everlasting light, and your God will be your glory! Seek His face, and He will be your beauty.

LORD, let me hope in You as my everlasting light. Clothe me with righteousness that You may be glorified. Use me to display Your beauty.

Please comfort me when I mourn; give me the oil of gladness instead of mourning, the garment of praise instead of a faint spirit; that I may be called an oak of righteousness, the planting of the LORD, that You may be glorified. Let me greatly rejoice in You; let my soul exult in my God, for You have clothed me with the garments of salvation; You have covered me with the robe of right-eousness, as a bride adorns herself with her jewels. As the earth brings forth its sprouts, and as a garden causes what is sown in it to sprout up, so cause righteousness and praise to sprout up before me. Amen (Isaiah 60 & 61).

*Even as the moon influences the tides of the sea, even so does prayer...influence the tides of godliness.* ~Charles Spurgeon

Author of all existence,

For my sake do not keep silent, and for my sake do not be quiet, until my righteousness goes forth as brightness, and my salvation as a burning torch. Let men see my righteousness, and women my glory, because You have called me by a new name that Your mouth has given. May I be as a crown of beauty in Your hand, and a royal diadem in the hand of my God. May You delight in Your servant. Fill me with the joyful knowledge that You take pleasure in me, that as the bridegroom rejoices over the bride, so You rejoice over me. Please establish me and make me a praise in the earth. Let those who eat the grain and drink the wine of my house praise the LORD, and exult in Your holiness.

O my soul, child of Zion, behold, your salvation has come; behold, His reward is Himself! Rejoice! For you are numbered among The Holy People, The Redeemed of the LORD; and you are called Sought Out, A Person Not Forsaken.

O Mighty One, help me to put my hope in You—You who are splendid in Your apparel, marching in the greatness of Your strength, speaking in righteousness, mighty to save. Thank You for sparing my lifeblood and bringing to me salvation by Your powerful arm. Thank You, that when I deserved to be trod in Your anger and trampled in Your wrath, You gave Christ to bear my punishment! I bless His name, for He is my joy and my salvation (Isaiah 62 & 63).

Source of all blessedness,

Let me be a person who recounts Your steadfast love, Your praises, according to all that You have given me, and the great goodness to my house that You have granted me according to Your compassion, according to the abundance of Your steadfast love. Thank You for becoming my Savior; that in Your love and in Your pity You have redeemed me, and lifted me up and carried me. Please continue to lead me, to make for Yourself a glorious name.

O my soul, it is my joy once again to remind you that He is your Father, though Abraham does not know you; He, the LORD, is your Father, your Redeemer from of old is His name!

O LORD, do not make me wander from Your ways and harden my heart, so that I fear You not. Keep me, and let me wait for You. For from of old no one has heard or perceived by the ear, no eye has seen a God besides You, who acts for those who wait for Him. You meet those who joyfully work righteousness—those who remember Your ways. Therefore may I present myself to You as a joyful servant of righteousness, remembering the ways of my God (Isaiah 63 & 64).

Praiseworthy LORD,

I am glad and rejoice forever in You; for behold, You made Your face to be my joy, and Your presence to be my gladness. Give me the assurance that You also rejoice in me and are glad in Your people.

Let me live by faith, hoping for the day when You create a new heavens and a new earth—when the sound of weeping and the cry of distress shall be heard no more, when Your chosen shall not labor in vain or bear children for calamity, when the wolf and the lamb shall graze together.

Guard me from the subtle deceitfulness of pride; help me to fight against arrogance. For this is the one to whom You will look: he who is humble and contrite in spirit and trembles at Your word.

Let me see Your glory and declare it among the nations, so that all flesh may know that You are the LORD and come to worship before You (Isaiah 65 & 66).

---

*"To encounter the words of the Scripture is to encounter God in action." We must not, therefore, pit theological truth against existential encounter. Rather, we must experience the truth.*
~Tim Keller

**I**nfinitely worthy LORD,

I will sing to You, for You have done glorious things; You have made Yourself my strength and my song, and You have become my salvation! You are my God, and I will praise You; You are the God of Jacob, and I will exalt You. Your right hand, O LORD, glorious in power, Your right hand, O LORD, shatters my enemies. In the greatness of Your majesty You overthrow my adversaries; You send out Your fury; it consumes them like stubble.

Who is like You, O LORD, among the gods? Who is like You, majestic in holiness, awesome in glorious deeds, doing wonders? You have led me, whom You have redeemed, in Your steadfast love; You have guided me by Your strength to Your holy abode. You alone will reign forever and ever.

I will sing to You, for You have triumphed gloriously over my enemies; You will guard and defend me, for You have become my salvation! (Exodus 15).

---

*What is the reason that some believers are so much brighter and holier than others? I believe the difference, nineteen cases out of twenty, arises from different habits about private prayer. I believe that those who are not eminently holy pray* little, *and those who are eminently holy pray* much. ~J. C. Ryle

Most blessed LORD,

Let me be a person who proclaims Your name and ascribes greatness to my God. For You are the Rock, whose work is perfect, for all Your ways are justice. A God of faithfulness and without iniquity, just and upright are You.

Keep me from becoming unmindful of the Rock that bore me, from forgetting the God who gave me birth. But make me remember and rejoice that You, even You, are my help, and there is no god beside You. You kill and You make alive; You wound and You heal; and there is none that can deliver out of Your hand.

Rejoice with Him, O my soul; bow down to Him, for He avenges the blood of His children and takes vengeance on His adversaries.

Most High God, let me dwell in safety; surround me all day long, and dwell between my shoulders. May I be blessed by You with favor, and be full of the blessing of the LORD. For there is none like You, who rides through the heavens to my help, through the skies in Your majesty. Be my dwelling place, and keep Your everlasting arms underneath me. Amen (Deuteronomy 32 & 33).

O Lord God,

Who am I, and what is my house, that You have given me such blessing? And yet this was a small thing in Your eyes, O Lord God. According to Your own heart You have brought me to Yourself, to make Your servant know Your abundant goodness. Therefore You are great, O Lord God. For there is none like You, and there is no God besides You.

I praise You that I am Your child, one of the people on earth whom You went to redeem to be Yours, making Yourself a name and doing for me great and awesome things. You established me for Yourself to be Yours forever. And You, O Lord, became my God.

And now, O Lord God, let Your name be magnified forever through me. Let me say, "The Lord of hosts is God over His people." Your promises are sure; You are my God, therefore Your servant has found courage to pray this prayer to You. May it please You to bless Your servant, so that I may continue forever before You. For only with Your blessing shall Your servant be blessed forever (II Samuel 7).

---

*The great fault of the children of God is,* they do not continue in prayer; they do not go on praying; they do not persevere. *If they desire anything for God's glory, they should pray until they get it. Oh, how good, and kind, and gracious, and condescending is the One with Whom we have to do! He has given me, unworthy as I am, immeasurably above all I had asked or thought!*
~George Mueller

Lord of Thunder,

Please be my rock and my fortress and my deliverer, my God, my rock, in whom I take refuge, my shield, and the horn of my salvation, my stronghold and my refuge, my savior; save me from violence. I call upon You, who are worthy to be praised, to plead for my perseverance.

When the waves of death encompass me, when the torrents of destruction assail me, let me hope in You. When the cords of Sheol entangle me, when the snares of death confront me, in my distress let me call upon You; may I call to my God. Hear my voice, and may my cry come to Your ears. Send from on high and take hold of me; draw me out of many waters. Rescue me and bring me out into a broad place; rescue me because You delight in me.

Enable me to keep Your ways and let me not wickedly depart from my God. May all Your rules be before me, and from Your statutes may I not turn aside. Make me blameless before You, and help me to keep myself from guilt. Mold me into a merciful, pure person, for with the merciful You show Yourself merciful; with the blameless person You show Yourself blameless; with the purified You deal purely, and with the crooked You make Yourself seem tortuous (II Samuel 22).

Savior of a humble people,

Be my lamp, O LORD, and lighten my darkness. Lead me in Your way, for Your way is perfect; Your word proves true; be a shield for me as I take refuge in You. For who is God but You? And who is a rock, except You? Therefore please be my strong refuge and make my way blameless. Make my feet like the feet of a deer and set me securely on the heights. Train my hands for war, so that I may use the shield of Your salvation.

By Your gentleness make me great. Give a wide place for my steps under me, and let my feet not slip. Equip me with strength for battle; make the evil that rises against me sink under me.

O my soul, the LORD lives, and blessed be our rock, and exalted be our God, the rock of our salvation!

For this we will praise You, O LORD, among the nations, and sing praises to Your name! Bring great salvation to me, and show steadfast love to me forever (II Samuel 22).

*The prayerless spirit saps a people's moral strength because it blunts their thought and conviction of the Holy. It must be so if prayer is such a moral blessing and such a shaping power, if it pass, by its nature, from the vague volume and passion of devotion to formed petition and effort. Prayerlessness is an injustice and a damage to our own soul, and therefore to its history, both in what we do and what we think. The root of all deadly heresy is prayerlessness.* ~P. T. Forsyth

God of Jacob,

Raise me up to live in the fear of You, so that I may dawn on my children like the morning light, like the sun shining forth on a cloudless morning, like rain that makes grass to sprout from the earth.

Thank You that You have shown great and steadfast love to me, and have caused me to walk before You in faithfulness, in righteousness, and in uprightness of heart toward You. Please keep for me this great and steadfast love.

Give me an understanding mind that I may discern between good and evil. Grant me a wise and discerning mind, so that I may walk in Your ways, keeping Your statutes and Your commandments. For there is no God like You, O LORD, in heaven above or on earth beneath, keeping covenant and showing steadfast love to Your servants who walk before You with all their heart. Behold, heaven and the highest heaven cannot contain You, yet have regard to the prayer of Your servant and his plea, O LORD, my God, listening to the cry and to the prayer that Your servant prays before You this day. Let me fear You all the days that I live, and may I shine forth the greatness of Your name, Your mighty hand, and Your outstretched arm (II Samuel 23, I Kings 3, 8).

---

*There are many good resources for learning how to pray, but the best way to learn how to pray is to pray.* ~Donald Whitney

Rock of Israel,

There is no God like You, in heaven above or on earth beneath, keeping covenant and steadfast love to Your servants who walk before You with all their heart. Therefore I ask that You would incline my heart to walk in Your ways, keeping Your statutes. Keep me in the way everlasting; let me pay close attention to my way, to walk before You as David walked before You. Listen to the plea of Your servant when I pray; hear from heaven and teach me the good way in which I should walk, and rain grace upon me that I may fear You all the days of my life.

Let Your eyes be open to my pleas, giving ear to me whenever I call You. For You chose me from among all the people of the earth to be Your heritage.

Blessed are You, O LORD, who has given rest to me. Not one word has failed of all Your good promise, which You spoke to Moses Your servant, which is mine in Christ Jesus! Be with me, and do not leave me or forsake me, that You may incline my heart to Yourself, to walk in all Your ways and to keep Your commandments, Your statutes, and Your rules. Maintain my cause, that all the peoples of the earth may know that the LORD is God; there is no other. Let my heart therefore be wholly true to You, my God, walking in Your statutes and keeping Your commandments (1 Kings 8).

O LORD the God of Israel,

Who is enthroned above the cherubim,

You are the God, You alone, of all the kingdoms of the earth; You have made heaven and earth. Incline Your ear; O LORD, and hear; open Your eyes, O LORD, and see; and hear the words of my prayer.

Let me give thanks to You; let me call upon Your name and make known Your deeds among the peoples! May I sing to You; let me sing praises to You and tell of all Your wonderful works! Cause me to glory in Your holy name; let my heart seek You and rejoice!

O my soul, chosen of Jacob, seek the LORD and His strength; seek His presence continually! Remember the wondrous works that He has done, His miracles and judgments He uttered.

LORD God, help me to remember Your covenant forever, the word that You commanded, for a thousand generations, the covenant that You made with Abraham. Let me sing to You with all the earth and tell of Your salvation from day to day! May I declare Your glory among the nations, Your marvelous works among all the peoples! For great are You, O LORD, and greatly to be praised, and You are to be held in awe above all gods. For all the gods of the peoples are idols, but You made the heavens. Splendor and majesty are before You; strength and joy are in Your place (II Kings 19 & I Chronicles 16).

God of my salvation,

Please increase my desire to ascribe to You glory and strength—to ascribe to You the glory due Your name and come humbly before You! Let me worship You in the splendor of holiness, trembling before You with joy. Let me be glad with the heavens, and rejoice with the earth, and let me say among the nations, "The LORD reigns!" Let me roar with the sea, and all that fills it; let me exult with the field, and everything in it! Then make me sing for joy with the trees of the forest before You, for You come to judge the earth.

O my soul, give thanks to the LORD, for He is good; for His steadfast love endures forever.

Keep me to the end, O God of my salvation, and deliver me from among the nations, that I may give thanks to Your holy name, and glory in Your praise. For blessed are You, the God of Israel, from everlasting to everlasting! Amen. Praise the LORD! (I Chronicles 16).

*The opposite of planning is the rut. If you don't plan a vacation you will probably stay home and watch TV. The natural, unplanned flow of spiritual life sinks to the lowest ebb of vitality. There is a race to be run and a fight to be fought. If you want renewal in your life of prayer you must* plan *to see it.*
~John Piper

Lord of all being,

Let Your eyes be open and Your ears attentive to the prayer of Your servant. And now arise, O LORD, and come to me. Clothe me with salvation, and make me rejoice in Your goodness. O LORD God, do not turn away the face of Your anointed one! Remember Your steadfast love for me, Your servant. Let me worship You and give thanks to You, saying, "For He is good, for His steadfast love endures forever."

May I continually humble myself, and pray and seek Your face and turn from wicked ways. Open Your eyes and let Your ears be attentive to me, for You have chosen and consecrated me that Your name may be exalted forever. Let me praise You as the God of heaven, who rules over all the kingdoms of the nations—as the God in whose hand are power and might, so that none is able to withstand You. May I give thanks to You, for Your steadfast love endures forever (II Chronicles 6 & 20).

**M**y God, the great, the mighty, and the awesome God,

O that I would delight myself in Your great goodness! Thank You that even when I forget You and stray from Your commandments, in Your great mercies You do not make an end of me or forsake me, for You are a gracious and merciful God.

When hardships befall me, let them not seem little to You; when I cry to You hear from heaven and deliver me according to Your mercies.

Be exalted in Your grace, for although I have acted wickedly, You have dealt faithfully.

Let me not boast in my wisdom, nor in my might, nor in my riches, but let me boast in this: that I understand and know You, that You are the LORD who practices steadfast love, and justice, and righteousness in the earth. For in these things You delight.

There is none like You, O LORD; You are great, and Your name is great in might. May I fear You, O King of the nations. For this is Your due; for among all the wise ones of the nations and in all their kingdoms there is none like You (Nehemiah 9, Jeremiah 9 & 10).

*As it is the business of tailors to make clothes and of cobblers to mend shoes, so it is the business of Christians to pray.*
~Martin Luther

Eternal God,

Let me rejoice in the Word, through whom all things were made. May I seek life only in Him.

Praise be to Your name for causing me to receive Him and believe on His name, for giving me the right to become Your child. Open my eyes to the glory of the Word, the glory of Your only Son, full of grace and truth. From His fullness let me receive grace upon grace—the grace and truth that come through Jesus Christ. Help me to do what is true and come to the light, so that it may be clearly seen that my deeds have been carried out in You.

Help me not to judge by appearances, but instead to judge with right judgment. And when I thirst, let me go to Christ and drink. Let me follow closely after Him always, so that I will not walk in darkness, but will have the light of life. Make me abide in His word as a true disciple so that I may know the truth and be set free by it (John 1 & 8).

Great Life-Giver,

May I never faint in following after my Shepherd's voice. Let Christ go before me and lead me, calling me by name and wooing me with His words.

Let me flee from the stranger, from the thief, and from the robber, for I do not know their voice.

I praise You that I have entered by Your Son into salvation and plentiful pasture. May I have life and have it abundantly in Him, for that is why He came. Let me trust Him always as my good Shepherd who lays down His life for sheep like me.

O my soul, trust Christ as your Shepherd! For His Father, who has given you to Him, is greater than all, and no one is able to snatch you out of Your Father's hand. And Christ and the Father are one (John 10).

*Nothing would do more to cure us of a belief in our own wisdom than the granting of some of our eager prayers. And nothing could humiliate us more than to have God say when the fulfillment of our desire brought leanness to our souls, "Well, you would have it." It is what He has said to many. But He has said more, "My grace is sufficient for thee." ~P. T. Forsyth*

Almighty Father,

Stir within me a stronger desire to glorify the Son of Man. Let me seek to glorify Him even in my death. For unless a grain of wheat falls into the earth and dies, it remains alone; but if it dies, it bears much fruit. And my desire is that I bear much fruit for the splendor of Your name. Therefore let me not love my life and so lose it, but help me to hate my life in this world so that I may keep it for eternal life. May I serve Christ and follow Christ, for then You will honor me.

Even in this very hour, Father, glorify Your name in me. Draw me to Yourself and let Christ always be my light, that I may not walk in darkness. Thank You that I have believed in the light and have become a child of light. I praise You that You did not blind my eyes or harden my heart so that I could not believe. But in grace You shone into my soul and made me to love the glory that comes from You more than the glory that comes from man (John 12).

Father of our Lord and Teacher,

Help me to persevere in washing the feet of others in all humility and joy. For Christ has given me an example, that I should also do as He has done. Assist me to do what I know as a servant, for a servant is not greater than his master.

Please deliver me from the treachery that still indwells me, for if You remove Your hand of grace I will surely betray Your Son. Spare me that dreadful end! Keep me faithful and steadfast in Jesus all my days, so that He may be glorified, and You will be glorified in Him.

Cause me to grow in love for others—to strive wholeheartedly to love others just as Christ has loved me, so that all people will know that I am His disciple, if I have love for others.

O my soul, let not your heart be troubled! Believe in God; believe also in Christ.

Father, fill me afresh with hope for the time when Your Son will come again and will take me to Himself, that where He is I may be also (John 13 & 14).

*Prayer is a special exercise of faith. Faith makes the prayer acceptable because it believes that either the prayer will be answered, or that something better will be given instead.*
~Martin Luther

Author of Pleasure,

All thanks and praise belong to You for showing me the way to Yourself, which is through Jesus alone. Blessed be Your glorious name for revealing Christ to me as the way, and the truth, and the life! May I grow to know Him better today than I did yesterday, which is to know You, His Father. I ask this only in Your Son's name, that You may be glorified in Him.

Create within me deeper love for Christ, and let this love constrain me to keep His commandments. Thank You for giving me another Helper to be with me forever, even the Spirit of truth, whom the world cannot receive, because it neither sees Him nor knows Him. Let me sing praise to You, for Your Spirit dwells in me.

O my soul, do not despair, for Christ has not left you as an orphan; He will come to you.

Father, may I love Christ and keep His words. By Your Holy Spirit, teach me all things and bring to my remembrance all that Christ has spoken. Grant His peace to me. Amen (John 14).

Sovereign Vinedresser,

Let not my heart be troubled, neither let it be afraid. Remind me that Christ is mighty to save, and You will not leave me or forsake me. Help me to do as You have commanded me, so that the world may know that I love You.

Please make me a branch that bears fruit because I abide in the vine, which is Christ. Prune me, that I may bear more fruit. Preserve me as one who abides in Christ and He in me, so that I bear much fruit, for apart from Christ I can do nothing.

O my soul, abide always in Jesus, with His words abiding in you. For then, when you ask whatever you wish, it will be done for you.

Father, glorify Yourself by making me bear much fruit, and so proving me to be Christ's disciple. May I abide in His love, for as You have loved Him, so has He loved me. Cause me to keep His commandments, for then I will abide in His love, just as He abides in Your love by keeping Your commandments.

Come quickly, Lord Jesus. Amen (John 14 & 15).

*Humbly I asked of God to give me joy,*
*To crown my life with blossoms of delight;*
*I pled for happiness without alloy,*
*Desiring that my pathway should be bright;*
*Prayerfully I sought these blessings to attain, —*
*And now I thank him that he gave me pain....*

*For with the pain and sorrow came to me*
*A dower of tenderness in act and thought;*
*And with the failure came a sympathy,*
*An insight that success had never bought.*
*Father, I had been foolish and unblest*
*If thou had granted me my blind request!*

~L. M. Montgomery

Everlasting God,

Thank You for choosing me and appointing me that I should go and bear fruit and that my fruit should abide. How gracious You are to call me Your friend! Fill me with love for my brothers and sisters in Christ.

If the world hates me, remind me that it hated Christ before it hated me. Prepare me to expect the world's hatred, for You chose me out of the world and I am no longer of the world. Help me to remember the word spoken by Christ: "A servant is not greater than his master," so that I will not be surprised or lose heart when persecution comes.

Let me persevere in bearing witness about Your glorious Son and enable me to do so by Your wonderful Helper, the Spirit of truth, who proceeds from You. May I herald the name of Jesus with boldness and joy.

In the midst of persecution, Father, keep me from falling away! May my heart not falter in unbelief (John 15).

**M**agnificent Father,

Now that Your Spirit of truth has come, let Him guide me into all the truth. May He glorify the Son by taking what is Christ's and declaring it to me. When I am sorrowful, turn my sorrow into joy. Fill me with hope that I will see Christ again soon, and then my heart will rejoice and no one will take my joy from me. Give me confidence to ask things of You in the name of Christ, for then I will receive, that my joy may be full. Imbue my soul with joy in Jesus! Cause me to listen to His words, that in Him I may have peace.

O my soul, in the world you will have tribulation. But take heart; Christ has overcome the world!

Father, grant me to know You, the only true God, and Jesus Christ more deeply, for that is eternal life. Enable me to glorify You on earth and accomplish the work that You have given me to do. Holy Father, keep us in Your name, that we may be one, even as You and Christ are one. Guard me so that I may never be lost. Open my ears to the words spoken by Your Son that I may have His joy fulfilled in myself. Thank You for giving us Your word through Christ! Amen (John 16 & 17).

*O what peace we often forfeit,*
*O what needless pain we bear,*
*All because we do not carry*
*Everything to God in prayer!*
*~Joseph Scriven*

God and Father of my Lord Jesus Christ,

Praise be to Your name because You have blessed me in Christ with every spiritual blessing in the heavenly places, even as You chose me in Him before the foundation of the world, that I should be holy and blameless before You. Please continue to sanctify me by the love with which You predestined me for adoption through Jesus Christ, according to the purpose of Your will, to the praise of Your glorious grace, with which You have blessed me in the Beloved. Worthy is He! How beautiful is Your Son! Let His name be exalted! For in Him I have redemption through His blood, the forgiveness of my trespasses, according to the riches of Your grace, which You lavished on me, in all wisdom and insight.

O my soul, let us laud His name together for His rich and lavish grace toward us! For in Christ we have obtained an inheritance, having been predestined according to the purpose of Him who works all things according to the counsel of His will, so that we who hope in Christ might be to the praise of His glory!

Father, remind me of my former state as a child of wrath by nature, like the rest of mankind, when I was dead in my trespasses and sins. Remind me of this so that I will rejoice afresh that You, being rich in mercy, because of the great love with which You loved me, even when I was dead in my trespasses, made me alive with Christ and saved me by grace. Continue showing me the immeasurable riches of Your grace in kindness toward me in Christ Jesus. Amen (Ephesians 1 & 2).

Mighty God,

Thank You for saving me by pure grace, so that I cannot boast as if it were my own doing, for my salvation is a gift of You and not a result of works. I praise Your name alone, because I am Your workmanship, created in Christ Jesus for good works. Therefore assist me to walk in the good works which You prepared beforehand for me.

Remind me constantly that I was at one time separated from Christ, having no hope and without God in the world. Remind me, so that I may rejoice continually that now in Christ Jesus I have been brought near by His blood. Fill me with the confidence that comes from knowing that Christ Himself is my peace—that He has reconciled me to You through the cross. Let me sing for joy anew because He has broken down the dividing wall of hostility between me and You—the one true and holy God.

In Christ please continue building us together into a dwelling place for Yourself by the Spirit. Amen (Ephesians 2).

---

*No tongue can express, no mind can reach, the heavenly placidness and soul-satisfying delight which are intimated in these words [Eph 2:18]. To come to God as a Father, through Christ, by the help and assistance of the Holy Spirit, revealing him as a Father unto us, and enabling us to go to him as a Father, how full of sweetness and satisfaction is it!*
~John Bunyan

God of revealed mystery,

O that I would be granted insight into the mystery of Christ by Your Spirit! Give me more and more depth of understanding of this marvelous mystery—that in Christ, through the gospel, I am a fellow heir with the commonwealth of Israel, a member of His body, and a partaker of the promise. By the working of Your power give me much grace to minister to those in need. Grant me more grace to love and spread the unsearchable riches of Christ, and to bring to light for many what is the plan of the mystery hidden for ages in You who created all things. Through me make known Your manifold wisdom.

Empower me to walk in a manner worthy of the calling to which I have been called, with all humility and gentleness, with patience, bearing with others in love, eager to maintain the unity of the Spirit in the bond of peace. Keep enlarging my heart and mind with the knowledge of Your Son, unto maturity, to the measure of the stature of the fullness of Christ, so that I may not be a child, tossed to and fro by the waves and carried about by every wind of doctrine. Guard me from human cunning, from craftiness in deceitful schemes. Enable me to speak the truth in love, to grow up in every way into Him who is the head, into Christ, and to work properly as a member of His body, helping to build it up in love (Ephesians 2 & 3).

Condescending God,

Prevent me from walking as the world does, in the futility of their minds. Do not let me live as one darkened in my understanding, hard of heart, callous, or greedy to practice every kind of impurity.

Instead, help me to put off my old self, which is corrupt through deceitful desires. Renew me in the spirit of my mind, and empower me to put on the new self, created after Your likeness in true righteousness and holiness. Make me put away falsehood and speak the truth with my neighbor.

When I am angry keep me from sin; grant me the grace not to let the sun go down on my anger. Let no corrupting talk come out of my mouth, but only such as is good for building up, as fits the occasion, that it may give grace to those who hear. And let me not grieve Your Holy Spirit, by whom I was sealed for the day of redemption. Put all bitterness and wrath and anger and clamor and slander away from me, along with all malice.

Grow me in kindness toward others, make me tenderhearted, so that I may be always forgiving others as You forgave me in Christ. Amen (Ephesians 4).

---

*The first reason why prayer leads to fullness of joy is that prayer is the nerve center of our fellowship with Jesus. He is not here physically to see. But in prayer we speak to Him just as though He were. And in the stillness of those sacred times, we listen to His Word and we pour out to Him our longings.*
~John Piper

Father of glory,

Assist me to be an imitator of You, as Your beloved child. And make me walk in love, as Christ loved me and gave Himself up for me, a fragrant offering and sacrifice to You.

Keep me from any form or appearance of sexual immorality and all impurity or covetousness. And let me guard my tongue, so that there might not be any filthiness or foolish talk or crude joking, which are out of place, but instead make me abound with thanksgiving.

Guide my feet to walk as a child of light, and enable me to discern what is pleasing to You. Let me take no part in the unfruitful works of darkness, but instead expose them. Open my eyes to look carefully how I walk, not as unwise but as wise, making the best use of the time, because the days are evil. Therefore help me to understand what Your will is.

Fill me with Your Spirit so that I may address others in psalms and hymns and spiritual songs, singing and making melody to You with all of my heart, giving thanks always and for everything to You in the name of the Lord Jesus Christ. And it is in His name that I come to You with this plea for grace. Amen (Ephesians 5).

*I do not understand prayer. Prayer is deeply personal and deeply mysterious. Adults try to figure out causation. Little children don't. They just ask.* ~Paul Miller

Sovereign LORD,

Shall I receive good from You, and shall I not receive evil? Therefore may I hold fast to my integrity when calamity comes. Instead of cursing, let me bless You saying, "The LORD gave, and the LORD has taken away; blessed be the name of the LORD." When evil befalls me, let me not charge You with wrong or sin with my lips. And when my suffering is great, enable me to find comfort in You.

May I seek You, and to You may I commit my cause. For You do great things and unsearchable, marvelous things without number: You set on high those who are lowly, and those who mourn are lifted up to safety. You save the needy from the sword of the mouth of the crafty and from the hand of the mighty.

O my soul, behold, your God is faithful when He wounds and shatters you even in your blamelessness. Therefore, do not despise His hard hand of grace, for He binds up, and His hands heal.

Father, deliver me from troubles! In famine redeem me from death, and in war from the power of the sword! Hide me from the lash of the tongue, and let me not fear destruction when it comes! (Job 1, 2, 4, 5).

---

*As prayer without faith is but a beating of the air, so trust without prayers [is] but a presumptuous bravado. He that promises to give, and bids us trust his promises, commands us to pray, and expects obedience to his commands. He will give, but not without our asking.* ~Thomas Lye

M erciful Almighty,

I am but of yesterday and know nothing, for my days on earth are a shadow. Therefore give wisdom to your servant and deal kindly with me that I might live uprightly. Please fill my mouth with laughter, and my lips with shouting. Let those who hate me be clothed with shame, for You are wise in heart and mighty in strength. You command the sun, and it does not rise; You seal up the stars; You alone stretched out the heavens and trampled the waves of the sea; You made the Bear and Orion, the Pleiades and the chambers of the south; You do great things beyond searching out, and marvelous things beyond number.

O how greatly and marvelously You have made me! And what a great marvel that You have saved me and kept me with the strength of Your right hand! Praise and glory are due Your name, for You have provided an arbiter between me and Yourself, even the man Jesus Christ, so that You have taken Your rod away from me, and Your dread no longer terrifies me. Therefore may I never loathe my life, or speak in bitterness of soul, for behold, I have an advocate with You, Jesus Christ the righteous (Job 8, 9, 10, I John 2).

Helper of the weak,

I give You praise and thanks, for Your hands fashioned and made me. You clothed me with skin and flesh, and knit me together with bones and sinews. You have granted me life and steadfast love, and Your care has preserved my spirit.

Therefore please do not destroy me altogether. Remember that You have made me like clay, and do not return me to the dust. Are not my days few? Therefore please bless me, and do not fill me with disgrace. Work wonders *for* me, and not against me.

Oh, that You would speak and open Your lips to me, and that You would tell me the secrets of wisdom! For You are manifold in understanding.

Know, my soul, that God exacts of you less than your guilt deserves, because of Christ. He has taken your guilt upon Himself, therefore be of good cheer and rejoice in the abundant life given you in Him!

Thank You, Father, that because of Your Son, I can lift up my face without blemish; I can be secure and not fear. Let my life be brighter than the noonday, and its darkness like the morning. May I feel secure, because there is hope—hope in Jesus. Let me lie down with none to make me afraid. Amen (Job 10 & 11).

*Prayer is the most tangible expression of trust in God.*
~Jerry Bridges

# Great God,

In whose hand is the life of every living thing and the breath of all mankind, with You are wisdom and might; You have counsel and understanding. Therefore, impart these things to me. Lead me with strength and sound wisdom. Let the eyes of my heart feast upon Your splendor. Let them brighten at the sight of Your justice, and with the vision of Your righteousness. For You overthrow the mighty. You uncover the deeps out of darkness and bring deep darkness to light. You make nations great, and You destroy them; You enlarge nations, and lead them away.

When Your majesty terrifies me, and the dread of You falls upon me, let me run to Christ. Even when I am a worthless physician in the day of my calamity, let me cling continually to Christ. And though You slay me, let me hope in You. Do not hide Your face or count me as Your enemy. Please do not frighten me or make me inherit the iniquities of my youth (Job 12 & 13).

*Prayer is the acknowledgment of God's sovereignty and of our dependence upon Him to act on our behalf. Prudence is the acknowledgment of our responsibility to use all legitimate means. We must not separate the two.* ~Jerry Bridges

**M**ajestic and mighty LORD,

Make me wise. Impart to me holy insight. And let me not do away with the fear of God, or hinder meditation before You. Keep my iniquity from teaching my mouth, and let me not choose the tongue of the crafty. Open my ears to listen to Your council, so that I do not limit wisdom to myself.

Protect me from the one who is abominable and corrupt, the man who drinks injustice like water. Let not distress and anguish terrify me; may they not prevail against me, for I have not trusted in emptiness, deceiving myself. Do not tear me with Your wrath or hate me, or gnash Your teeth at me. Neither give me up to the ungodly or cast me into the hands of the wicked. Please do not break me apart, or seize me by the neck and dash me to pieces, or set me up as Your target, surrounding me with Your archers. Do not break me with breach upon breach, or run upon me like a warrior. For even though I deserve all these things, spare me because of Christ, for I abide in Him.

O my soul, hope continually in Christ! Look to Him alone for your salvation. Even now, behold, your witness is in heaven, and He who testifies for you is on high. He argues your case with God, as a son of man does with his neighbor.

O Father I offer You praise and thanks for the advocate You have given me in Jesus! (Job 15 & 16).

Restorer of the broken in spirit,

Even when I make my bed in darkness, when reproach is cast upon me, when You strip my glory from me, and set darkness upon my paths, when my relatives fail me, and close friends forget me, when my intimate friends abhor me and those whom I love turn against me, let me hope in Christ. For He lives, and has stood upon the earth, and I shall see Him for myself. My eyes shall behold Him! May I long for that day and not lose heart.

Because I am found in Christ, let my children dance. Let them sing to the tambourine and the lyre and rejoice to the sound of the pipe. May they spend their days in prosperity. Let me receive instruction from Your Son's mouth, and lay up His words in my heart. Cause me to turn always to You so that I will be built up, and remove injustice far from my house.

O my soul, if you lay gold in the dust, and gold of Ophir among the stones of the torrent bed, then the Almighty will be your gold and your precious silver. For then you will delight yourself in the Almighty and lift up your face to God.

When I pray to You, hear me, and make light to shine on my ways. Be exalted! For You deliver me even though I am not innocent, and will grant me cleanness of hands (Job 17, 19, 21, 22).

*Whether we like it or not, asking is the rule of the Kingdom.*
*~Charles Spurgeon*

Righteous Judge,

Thank You that Christ comes even to Your seat and lays my case before You. He alone is the upright man who can argue on my behalf so that I am acquitted forever by my Judge.

Behold, You know the way that I take; when You have tried me, let me come out as gold. Make my foot hold fast to Your steps; keep me in Your way and do not let me turn aside. Let me never depart from the commandment of Your lips; may I treasure the words of Your mouth more than my portion of food.

You are unchangeable, and who can turn You back? What You desire, do so in me. Complete what You have appointed for me. Even if You must terrify me and make my heart faint, let me hope in Your steadfast love. May I trust Your hand when thick darkness covers my face. Amen (Job 23).

*We must combine tenacious importunity, a "striving with God," with deep acceptance of God's wise will, whatever it is.*
~Tim Keller

God of dominion,

Is there any number to Your armies? Upon whom does Your light not arise? Thank You, that because of Christ, I am in the right before You. Be praised! For I who am born of man have Him as my purity. His hand pierced the fleeing serpent, and by His spirit I have been made fair.

O my soul, adore and fear your God. He stretches out the north over the void and hangs the earth on nothing. The pillars of heaven tremble and are astounded at His rebuke. By His power He stilled the sea; by His understanding He shattered Rahab, the terror of the deep. Behold, these are but the outskirts of His ways, and how small a whisper do we hear of Him!

Father, as long as my breath is in me, and Your spirit is in my nostrils, keep my lips from speaking falsehood, and my tongue from uttering deceit. Let me hold fast to Christ's righteousness and not let it go.

Grant me wisdom. For You alone understand the way to it, and know its place. You said, "Behold, the fear of the Lord, that is wisdom, and to turn away from evil is understanding." Therefore increase my fear of You; let me turn away from evil and gain a discerning heart (Job 25-28).

Wise Almighty,

Oh, that You might watch over me, making Your lamp to shine upon my head, so that by Your light I may walk through darkness. Let Your friendship be upon my house, and stay always with me.

Keep my children all around me; may my steps be washed with blessing, and cause the rock to pour out for me streams of oil. Make me one who delivers the poor who cry for help, and the fatherless who have none to help them, so that when the ear hears of me, it will call me blessed, and when the eye sees me, it will approve,

Mold me into someone upon whom come the blessings of those who are about to perish, and may I cause the widow's heart to sing for joy. Put righteousness on me and clothe me with it; make my justice like a robe and a turban.

Let me be eyes to the blind, feet to the lame, and father to the needy. Let me search out the cause of even the one whom I do not know. Use me to break the fangs of the unrighteous and make them drop their prey from their teeth (Job 29).

*An attitude of acceptance says that we trust God, that He loves us, and knows what is best for us. Acceptance does not mean that we do not pray for physical healing, or for the conception and birth of a little one to our marriage. We should indeed pray for those things, but we should pray in a trusting way. We should realize that, though God can do all things, for infinitely wise and loving reasons, He may not do that which we pray that He will do. How do we know how long to pray? As long as we can pray trustingly, with an attitude of acceptance of His will, we should pray as long as the desire remains.*
~Jerry Bridges

God of justice and righteousness,

Make me wise. Fill me with understanding so that people will listen to me and wait and keep silence for my counsel—that they may wait for me as for the rain and open their mouths as for the spring rain.

Let me not despair when my soul is poured out within me, when days of affliction have taken hold of me. When I am cast into the mire, and have become like dust and ashes, let me cry to You for help, and answer me. Even when You seem to have turned cruel to me, may I hope in Your promise; may I wait for Your unfailing love. Let me be a person who weeps for those whose days are hard, and whose soul grieves for the needy.

Assist me to comfort others when evil comes; when they have waited for light, but darkness comes. Grant me wisdom and compassion to bear their turmoil with them; to encourage them when days of affliction come to meet them. Be merciful to me, for I have not walked with falsehood and my foot has not hastened to deceit (Job 30).

**M**ajestic LORD,

Keep me from making gold my trust or calling fine gold my confidence. Let me not rejoice only because my wealth is abundant or because my hand has found much. Guard my heart from being secretly enticed to worship the shining splendor of what has been made, for that would be false to You. May I not rejoice at the ruin of the one who hates me, or exult when evil overtakes him. Let not my mouth sin by asking for his life with a curse.

Sanctify me so that I may be able to say that the sojourner has not lodged in the street, that I have opened my doors to the traveler, that I have withheld nothing that the poor desired, and have not caused the eyes of the widow to fail, that I have not left the fatherless hungry. Keep me from concealing my transgressions as others do by hiding iniquity in my bosom.

O my soul, behold, you are toward God as everyone else; you too were pinched off from a piece of clay. Cling to Christ as your righteousness, for He is pure, without transgression; He is clean, and there is no iniquity in Him (Job 31 & 33).

*Intercessory prayer is the purifying bath into which the individual and the fellowship must enter every day.*
~Dietrich Bonhoeffer

O God, who is greater than man,

Let me hope in Christ when my soul draws near the pit, and my life to those who bring death. May my flesh become fresh with youth; let me return to the days of my youthful vigor. When I pray to You, please accept me; may I see Your face with a shout of joy, as You restore to me my righteousness.

O my soul, sing before men and say, "I sinned and perverted what was right, and it was not repaid to me. The LORD has redeemed me from going down into the pit, and my life shall look upon the light."

Do all these things with me, O Father, to bring back my soul from the pit, that I may be lighted with the light of life.

Listen to me; hear my words and give ear to me. Please teach me wisdom. Thank You that I do not drink up scoffing like water, that You have kept me from being a person who travels in company with evildoers or walks with wicked men. May I never say, "It profits a man nothing that he should take delight in God," for such are the words of the wicked (Job 33 & 34).

*True, whole prayer is nothing but love.* ~St. Augustine

O Father, perfect in knowledge,

Be praised among the nations! For You are mighty in strength and understanding. Do not despise me; when I am afflicted please give me my right and keep me alive. Do not withdraw Your eyes from me.

Open my ears to instruction and help me to return from iniquity. May I listen and serve You, and complete my days in prosperity, and my years in pleasantness. Let me not cherish anger as the godless in heart. Deliver me by my affliction and open my ear by adversity. Allure me out of distress into a broad place, and may what is set on my table be full of fatness.

O my soul, behold, God is exalted in His power; who is a teacher like Him? Who has prescribed for Him His way, or who can say, "You have done wrong?" Remember to extol His work, of which men have sung. Behold, God is great, and we know Him not, the number of His years is unsearchable. For He draws up the drops of water; they distill His mist in rain which the skies pour down and drop on mankind abundantly. Can anyone understand the spreading of the clouds, the thunderings of His pavilion? Behold, He scatters His lightning about Him and covers the roots of the sea. For by these He judges peoples; He gives food in abundance. He covers His hands with the lightning and commands it to strike the mark. Its crashing declares His presence; the cattle also declare that He rises (Job 36).

God of thunderous majesty,

Let me sing of Your power; when I see it let my heart tremble and leap out of its place. For You thunder wondrously with Your voice; You do great things that we cannot comprehend. May I bow before You when I behold the strength of Your word, for to the snow You say, "Fall on the earth," likewise to the downpour, Your mighty downpour. May I worship You with a reverent heart, for by Your breath ice is given, and the broad waters are frozen fast. Let my heart tremble before You in wonder, for You load the thick cloud with moisture; the clouds scatter Your lightning. They turn around and around by Your guidance, to accomplish all that You command them on the face of the habitable world. Whether for correction or for Your land or for love, You cause it to happen.

Hear me, O my soul; stop and consider the wondrous works of God.

Lord, I praise You for Your wondrous works—the rain, the lightning, the wind, the clouds; they declare the glory of Him who is perfect in knowledge.

May I worship You as I look on the light when it is bright in the skies, when the wind has passed and cleared them. Out of the north comes golden splendor; You are clothed with awesome majesty. Let me praise You as the One great in power, in justice, and abundant in righteousness. Therefore, let me fear You. Amen (Job 37).

Father of my Lord Jesus Christ,

According to Your foreknowledge, in the sanctification of the Spirit, for obedience to Jesus Christ and for sprinkling with His blood: please multiply grace and peace to me.

Let me bless You, for according to Your great mercy, You have caused me to be born again to a living hope through the resurrection of Jesus Christ from the dead, to an inheritance that is imperishable, undefiled, and unfading, kept in heaven for me. Thank You that by Your power I am being guarded through faith for a salvation ready to be revealed in the last time. Let me rejoice in this. May I rejoice even when it is necessary that I be grieved for a little while by various trials, so that the tested genuineness of my faith—more precious than gold that perishes though it is tested by fire—may be found to result in praise and glory and honor at the revelation of Jesus Christ. Though I have not seen Him, let me love Him all the more. Though I do not now see Him, I praise You that I believe in Him and rejoice with joy that is inexpressible and filled with glory, obtaining the outcome of my faith, the salvation of my soul (I Peter 1).

*Prayer does not fit us for the greater work,
prayer is the greater work.*
~Oswald Chambers

Father of our living hope,

O that You would assist me to prepare my mind for action, and to be sober-minded. Let me set my hope fully on the grace that will be brought to me at the revelation of Jesus Christ. As an obedient child, may I not be conformed to the passions of my former ignorance. Instead, as You who called me are holy, make me holy in all my conduct, since it is written, "You shall be holy, for I am holy." And since You are my Father who judges impartially according to my deeds, cause me to conduct myself with fear throughout the time of my exile on this earth, knowing that I was ransomed from the futile ways inherited from my forefathers, not with perishable things such as silver or gold, but with the precious blood of Christ, like that of a lamb without blemish or spot.

O my soul, He was made manifest in the last times for your sake, for through Him you are a believer in God, who raised Him from the dead and gave Him glory, so that your faith and hope are in God.

Enable me, O LORD, to purify my soul by my obedience to the truth for a sincere love, so that I may love others earnestly from a pure heart, since I have been born again, not of perishable seed but of imperishable, through Your living and abiding word. Praise be to Your name! For this word is the good news that was preached to me. Amen (I Peter 1).

Eternal LORD,

By Your mighty Spirit enable me to put away all malice and all deceit and hypocrisy and envy and all slander. Make me long for the pure spiritual milk, that by it I may grow up to salvation—since indeed I have tasted that You are good.

Thank You that as I come to Christ, a living stone rejected by men but in Your sight chosen and precious, I am being built up like a living stone into a spiritual house to be part of a holy priesthood, to offer spiritual sacrifices acceptable to You through Jesus Christ.

I praise You that I am part of Your chosen race, Your royal priesthood, Your holy nation, and a people for Your own possession. And because I am, let me ever proclaim Your excellencies—for You are the God who has called me out of darkness into Your marvelous light. Thank You that although I once was not of a people, now I am of Your people; once I had not received mercy, but now I have received mercy.

My soul, I urge you as a sojourner and exile to abstain from the passions of the flesh, which wage war against your soul.

Father, keep my conduct among the Gentiles honorable, so that when they speak against me as an evildoer, they may see my good deeds and glorify You on the day of visitation (I Peter 2).

*To clasp the hands in prayer is the beginning of an uprising against the disorder of the world.* ~Karl Barth

Lord of unbounded mercy,

Help me to live as one who is free, not using my freedom as a cover-up for evil, but living as Your bondservant. Let me honor everyone, love the brother-hood, fear You, and honor the governing authorities.

Grant me the grace to endure sorrows while suffering unjustly, being mindful of You. For if when I do good and suffer for it I endure, this is a gracious thing in Your sight.

For to this I have been called, because Christ also suffered for me leaving an example, so that I might follow in His steps. He committed no sin, neither was deceit found in His mouth.

O God, make me like Him, so that when I am reviled, I will not revile in return. When I suffer, let me not threaten, but continue entrusting myself to You who judge justly. Thank You that I have a perfect example in Christ Jesus! He himself bore my sins in His body on the tree, that I might die to sin and live to righteousness. May He be exalted! For by His wounds I have been healed. Thank You, that even though I was straying like a sheep, now I have returned to You, the Shepherd and Overseer of my soul. Amen (I Peter 2).

*Everyone talks now about how prayer is relationship, but often what people mean is having warm fuzzies with God. Nothing wrong with warm fuzzies, but relationships are far richer and more complex.* ~Paul Miller

You who have called us to Your eternal glory in Christ,

Do not let me repay evil for evil or reviling for reviling, but on the contrary, may I bless, for to this I was called, that I may obtain a blessing. I desire to love life and see good days, therefore keep my tongue from evil and my lips from speaking deceit; let me turn away from evil and do good; let me seek peace and pursue it. For Your eyes are on the righteous, and Your ears are open to their prayer. But Your face is against those who do evil.

O my soul, even if you should suffer for righteousness' sake, you will be blessed. Rejoice, and have no fear of man, nor be troubled.

Father, may I regard Christ the Lord as holy in my heart, and always be prepared to make a defense to anyone who asks me for a reason for the hope that is in me. Let me do it with gentleness and respect, having a good conscience, so that, when I am slandered, those who revile my good behavior in Christ may be put to shame (I Peter 3).

*God delights in the aroma of his own glory
as he smells it in the prayers of his people.* ~John Piper

God of all Grace,

If I am insulted for the name of Christ, let me take comfort in the truth that I am blessed, because the Spirit of glory and of God rests upon me. If I suffer as a Christian, let me not be ashamed, but let me glorify You in that name. Indeed, when I suffer according to Your will, let me entrust my soul to You—my faithful Creator—while doing good.

Let me not be surprised at the fiery trial when it comes upon me to test me, as though something strange were happening to me. But make me rejoice insofar as I share Christ's sufferings, that I may also rejoice and be glad when His glory is revealed.

Father, help me to lead and guide others whom You have entrusted me, not under compulsion, but eagerly and joyfully, as You would have me; not domineering over them, but being an example. Please clothe me with humility toward others, for You oppose the proud but give grace to the humble. I want *You*. I need Your grace. Humble me, therefore, under Your mighty hand so that at the proper time You may exalt me. I cast my anxieties on You, because You care for me. Make me sober-minded. May I be watchful. Enable me to resist my adversary the devil firm in my faith, and remind me that the same kinds of suffering are being experienced by my brotherhood throughout the world. And when I have suffered a little while, restore, confirm, strengthen, and establish me. To You be the dominion forever and ever. Amen (I Peter 4 & 5).

Compassionate Father,

May grace and peace be multiplied to me in the knowledge of You and of Jesus my Lord. Thank You that Your divine power has granted to me all things that pertain to life and godliness, through the knowledge of You who called us to Your own glory and excellence, by which You have granted to me Your precious and very great promises, so that through them I may become a partaker of the divine nature, having escaped from the corruption that is in the world because of sinful desire.

Because of this great blessing, help me to make every effort to supplement my faith with virtue, and virtue with knowledge, and knowledge with self-control, and self-control with steadfastness, and steadfastness with godliness, and godliness with brotherly affection, and brotherly affection with love. Make these qualities my own and let them increase in me, to keep me from being ineffective or unfruitful in the knowledge of my Lord Jesus Christ. May I never be so nearsighted as to be blind, forgetting that I was cleansed from my former sins. Therefore, assist me to be all the more diligent to make my calling and election sure, for if I practice these qualities I will never fall. Please uphold me! And richly provide for me an entrance into the eternal kingdom of our Lord and Savior Jesus Christ. Hasten the coming of His kingdom, I pray. Amen (II Peter 1).

*Prayer is the power that wields the weapon of the Word; but the Word itself is the weapon by which the nations will be brought to faith and obedience.* ~John Piper

Faithful King,

Make me the sort of person who lives a life of holiness and godliness, waiting for and hastening the coming of the day of God, because of which the heavens will be set on fire and dissolved, and the heavenly bodies will melt as they burn. While I wait for a new heavens and a new earth in which righteousness dwells, let me be diligent to be found by You without spot or blemish, and at peace.

Protect me from false teachers that will rise up and secretly bring destructive heresies. Let me not be found among the many who will follow their sensuality and blaspheme the way of truth. Keep me far from the way of the unrighteous, who speak loud boasts of folly and are slaves to corruption. May it never be that after I have escaped the defilements of the world through the knowledge of my Lord and Savior Jesus Christ, I am again entangled in them and overcome! Guard me from such a fate, for my last state would become worse for me than the first.

Therefore, help me to take care that I am not carried away with the error of lawless people and so lose my own stability. But cause me to grow in the grace and knowledge of my Lord and Savior Jesus Christ.

To You be the glory both now and to the day of eternity. Amen (II Peter 2 & 3).

Father,

Let whatever happens to me serve to advance the gospel, so that even my suffering and imprisonment may magnify Christ. May my life be a source of confidence for others in You, that makes them much more bold to speak the word without fear.

Keep me from proclaiming Christ out of envy or rivalry, and instead let me do so from good will and out of love. More than that, let me rejoice in Christ, and in His truth proclaimed. And help me to continue stirring up others for their progress and joy in the faith.

Please let my manner of life be worthy of the gospel of Christ, so that I may stand firm in one spirit, with one mind striving for the faith of the gospel, and not frightened in anything by my opponents. Thank you that it has been granted to me that for the sake of Christ I should not only believe in Him but also suffer for His sake.

Fill me with the joy of being of the same mind with others, having the same love, being in full accord and of one mind. Keep me from doing anything from rivalry or conceit, but let me in humility count others more significant than myself. Let me look not only to my own interests, but also to the interests of others, having the very mind of Christ. Amen (Philippians 1 & 2).

*The true theology is warm, and it steams upward into prayer.*
~P.T. Forsyth

Highly exalted God,

Please grow me into a person who does all things without grumbling or questioning, that I may be blameless and innocent, a child of God without blemish in the midst of a crooked and twisted generation. Let me shine as a light in the world, holding fast to the word of life, so that in the day of Christ I may be proud that I did not pray in vain or find encouragement in vain. Enable me to rejoice and be glad to suffer for the sake of others—even to pour out my life as a drink offering upon the sacrificial offering of my faith. Likewise let me also be glad and rejoice to endure hardship for the name of Christ. Make me genuinely concerned for the welfare of others, seeking not my own interests but those of Jesus Christ.

Help me to look out for the dogs, for the evildoers, and for those who put confidence in their works. Help me to remain steadfast in worship by Your Spirit, glorying in Christ Jesus, and putting no confidence in the flesh. More than anything, strengthen me to forget what lies behind and strain forward to what lies ahead, and press on toward the goal for the prize of Your upward call in Christ Jesus. Let me also hold true to what I have attained. Amen (Philippians 2 & 3).

Great Savior,

Thank you that my citizenship is in heaven! Therefore let me not set my mind on earthly things, but instead await a Savior, the Lord Jesus Christ, who will transform my lowly body to be like His glorious body, by the power that enables Him even to subject all things to Himself.

Therefore, my soul, stand firm in the Lord. Rejoice in the Lord always; again I will say, Rejoice!

Father, teach me how to be content in every situation. Help me to know how to be brought low, and how to abound. In any and every circumstance show me the secret of facing plenty and hunger, abundance and need. Strengthen me to do all things through You. Please supply every need of mine according to Your riches in glory in Christ Jesus. To You, our God and Father, be glory forever and ever! May the grace of the Lord Jesus Christ be with my spirit. Amen (Philippians 3 & 4).

*When you encounter trial and suffering, what's the content of your prayer? If yours is primarily a plea for relief from suffering, then please know that this is biblical. It's certainly not unbiblical. We're encouraged by God in Scripture to pray for relief from suffering. But this should never be the exclusive focus of our prayers in those times. ~C.J. Mahaney*

Sovereign LORD of Zion,

Let me sing aloud and shout! May I rejoice and exult with all my heart as a child of Jerusalem. For You have taken away the judgments against me because of Christ. You have cleared away my enemies—death, sin, and Satan. Let me never again fear evil, for You—the King of Israel, the LORD—are near me. May I not fear, and let not my hands grow weak.

O my soul, the LORD your God is with you, a mighty one who will save; He rejoices over you with gladness; He quiets you by His love; He exults over You with loud singing.

LORD God, when I mourn, please gather me and bring me to Your festival, so that I will no longer suffer reproach. Deal with all my oppressors. Change my shame into praise and renown in all the earth. Restore my fortunes so that You will be renowned and praised among all the peoples of the earth (Zephaniah 3).

*Restraining pray'r, we cease to fight;*
*Pray'r makes the Christian's armour bright.*
~William Cowper

God my Savior,

Thank You for Christ Jesus my hope. Watch over me and guard me from those who teach any different doctrine, or devote themselves to myths, who promote speculations rather than the good order from You that is by faith. And as you protect me, fill me with the love that issues from a pure heart and a good conscience and a sincere faith. Let me not swerve from these, or wander away into vain discussion.

I thank You, Christ Jesus my Lord, for giving me strength, and because You judged me faithful, appointing me to Your service, though formerly I was so unworthy.

O my soul, rejoice! Remember that you received mercy, and the grace of our Lord overflowed for you with the faith and love that are in Christ Jesus.

I praise You, Father, for showing me mercy, so that in me Jesus Christ might display His perfect patience as an example to those who are to believe in Him for eternal life.

To You, the King of ages, immortal, invisible, the only God, be honor and glory forever and ever! Amen (I Timothy 1).

---

*There is nothing so abnormal, so unworldly, so supernatural, in human life as prayer.... The whole Christian life in so far as it is lived from the Cross and by the Cross is rationally an extravagance.* ~P.T. Forsyth

Mighty LORD,

I entrust myself entirely to Your charge and care, in accordance with Your grace in Christ Jesus toward me. By Your power may I wage the good warfare, holding faith and a good conscience. Let me never make shipwreck of my faith!

Protect me from those who depart from the faith by devoting themselves to deceitful spirits and teachings of demons. Let me have nothing to do with irreverent, silly myths. Rather train me for godliness, for while bodily training is of some value, godliness is of value in every way, as it holds promise for the present life and also for the life to come.

May I toil and strive to this end, because I have my hope set on You, the living God (I Timothy 1, 2, 4).

*If we do not abide in prayer,
we shall abide in cursed temptations.* ~John Owen

Savior of the weak,

Let me set an example for believers in speech, in conduct, in love, in faith, in purity. Make me find full delight in the sound words of my Lord Jesus Christ and the teaching that accords with godliness. And keep me from an unhealthy craving for controversy and for quarrels about words. Let me instead pursue godliness with contentment, for therein there is great gain.

May I be content that I have food and clothing, and let me not desire to be rich, for those who desire to be rich fall into temptation, into a snare, into many senseless and harmful desires that plunge people into ruin and destruction.

Father, guard me from craving riches! For the love of money is a root of all kinds of evil. Keep me from the fate of those who, through this craving, have wandered away from the faith and pierced themselves with many pangs.

Let my love and craving be for Christ (I Timothy 4 & 6).

*For, as for my heart, when I go to pray, I find it so loth to go to God, and when it is with him, so loth to stay with him, that many times I am forced in my Prayers; first to beg God that he would take mine heart, and set it on himself in Christ, and when it is there, that he would keep it there (Psalm 86.11).*
~John Bunyan

Father of glory,

As for me, let me flee from the desire to be rich and the love of money. Help and enable me to pursue with renewed vigor righteousness, godliness, faith, love, steadfastness, and gentleness. Strengthen me to fight the good fight of the faith, and to take hold of the eternal life to which I was called.

O my soul, I charge you in the presence of God, who gives life to all things, and of Christ Jesus, to keep your conduct unstained and free from reproach until the appearing of the Lord Jesus Christ, which He will display at the proper time—He who is the blessed and only Sovereign, the King of kings and Lord of lords, who alone has immortality, who dwells in unapproachable light, whom no one has ever seen or can see.

To You, O God, be honor and eternal dominion! If You bless me with plenty, let me never become haughty or set my hopes on the uncertainty of riches. Rather cause me to set my hopes on You—the One who richly provides me with everything to enjoy. Help me to do good, to be rich in good works, to be generous and ready to share, thus storing up treasure for myself as a good foundation for the future so that I may take hold of that which is truly life (I Timothy 6).

God and Father,

May grace, mercy, and peace be multiplied to me. Please grow my faith in sincerity. Fan into flame the gifts You have given me, and remind me that You gave me a spirit not of fear but of power and love and self-control.

Therefore let me not be ashamed of the testimony about my Lord, but by Your power cause me to rejoice to share in suffering for the gospel. For You are the one who saved me and called me to a holy calling, not because of my works but because of Your own purpose and grace, which You gave me in Christ Jesus before the ages began. Thank You that He is my Savior, even He who abolished death and brought life and immortality to light through the gospel. Let me not be ashamed to suffer for this gospel, for I know whom I have believed. Convince me that You are able to guard what has been entrusted to me until that Day.

Help me to follow the pattern of the sound words that I have heard from the Scriptures, in the faith and love that are in Christ Jesus. By the Holy Spirit who dwells within me, may I guard the good deposit entrusted to me (II Timothy 1).

*It is not well for a man to pray cream and live skim milk.*
*~Henry Ward Beecher*

Father in heaven,

Please strengthen me by the grace that is in Christ Jesus, so that I may be able to share in suffering as His good soldier. May I constantly remember Jesus Christ, risen from the dead, the offspring of David. Let me rejoice to endure everything for the sake of the elect, that they also may obtain the salvation that is in Christ Jesus with eternal glory.

O my soul, the saying is trustworthy, for: If we have died with Him, we will also live with Him; if we endure, we will also reign with Him; if we deny Him, He also will deny us; if we are faithless, He remains faithful—for He cannot deny Himself.

O God, remind me of these things. Compel me to do my best to present myself to You as one approved, a worker who has no need to be ashamed, rightly handling the word of truth. May I avoid irreverent babble, for it will lead people into more and more ungodliness, and their talk will spread like gangrene. Thank You that Your firm foundation stands, bearing this seal: "The Lord knows those who are His," and "Let everyone who names the name of the Lord depart from iniquity" (II Timothy 2).

*Were it not for the Spirit, none would be able to persevere in prayer. 'A man without the help of the Spirit', John Bunyan once declared, 'cannot so much as pray once; much less, continue...in a sweet praying frame.' It needs to be noted that, for all who persevere in this struggle and discipline of prayer, there are times of exquisite delight when the struggle, and duty slides over into pure joy.* ~Michael A. G. Haykin

# Holy Master,

Let me cleanse myself from what is dishonorable so that I will be a vessel for honorable use, set apart as holy, useful to You, ready for every good work.

Make me flee youthful passions and pursue righteousness, faith, love, and peace, along with those who call on the Lord from a pure heart. May I have nothing to do with foolish, ignorant controversies, since they breed quarrels. Let me not be quarrelsome but kind to everyone.

Help me to patiently endure evil. Protect me from those who are lovers of self, lovers of money, proud, arrogant, abusive, disobedient to their parents, ungrateful, unholy, heartless, unappeasable, slanderous, without self-control, brutal, not loving good, treacherous, reckless, swollen with conceit, lovers of pleasure rather than lovers of You, having the appearance of godliness, but denying its power. Help me to avoid such people.

Enable me to lead righteously in my teaching, my conduct, my aim in life, my faith, my patience, my love, my steadfastness, and my persecutions and sufferings.

Indeed, my soul, let me remind you that all who desire to live a godly life in Christ Jesus will be persecuted, while evil people and imposters will go on from bad to worse, deceiving and being deceived.

But as for me, Lord God, may I continue in what I have learned and have firmly believed, becoming more and more acquainted with the sacred writings, which are able to make me wise for salvation through faith in Christ Jesus. Increase my love for Scripture. May what You have breathed out teach me, reprove me, correct me, and train me in righteousness, that I may be competent, equipped for every good work (II Timothy 2 & 3).

※

*My simple exhortation is this: Let us take time this very day to rethink our priorities and how prayer fits in. Make some new resolve. Try some new venture with God. Set a time. Set a place. Choose a portion of Scripture to guide you. Don't be tyrannized by the press of busy days. We all need midcourse corrections. Make this a day of turning to prayer—for the glory of God and for the fullness of your joy.*
~John Piper

God and Father of Christ Jesus,

Who is to judge the living and the dead, may I delight in and spread Your word all the more. Make me ready to bear witness to Christ's appearing and His kingdom in season and out of season. Let me reprove, rebuke, and exhort my brothers in Christ with complete patience and teaching.

Guard me from becoming a person who will not endure sound teaching—one who, having itching ears, accumulates for himself teachers to suit his own passions, and turns away from listening to the truth and wanders off into myths. May it never be! Instead, keep me always sober-minded. Enable me to endure suffering, to do the work of an evangelist, and to fulfill the ministry to which You have called me.

O Father, please strengthen me to fight the good fight. Carry me onward to finish the race. Keep me so that I might keep the faith. Make my heart love Christ's appearing all the more, so that there may be laid up for me the crown of righteousness, which He, the righteous judge, will award to me on that Day.

May Christ Jesus and His grace be with my spirit. Amen (II Timothy 4).

*May God give us a heart and a will to make prayer, prayer for the exaltation of God and extension of the kingdom, a daily reality in our lives.* ~Michael A. G. Haykin

# Appendix
## Books Quoted

Bounds, E.M. *Man of Prayer*
Bridges, Jerry. *Trusting God: Even When Life Hurts*
Brother Lawrence. *The Practice of the Presence of God*
Buttrick, George A. *Prayer*
Carson, D.A. *Call to Spiritual Reformation: Priorities from Paul and His Prayers*
Di Gangi, Marioano. *A Golden Treasury of Puritan Devotions*
Dubay, Thomas. *The Evidential Power of Beauty*
Edwards, Jonathan. *Religious Affections*
Edwards, Jonathan. *The Works of Jonathan Edwards, Vol. 2*
Forsyth, P.T. *The Soul of Prayer*
Grudem, Wayne. *Systematic Theology*
Haykin, Michael. *The God Who Draws Near*
Hosier, Helen. *Jonathan Edwards: The Great Awakener*
Keller, Timothy. *Prayer: Experiencing Awe and Intimacy with God*
Mahaney, C.J. *Humility: True Greatness*
Mason, Mike. *Practicing the Presence of People*
Mason, Mike. *The Gospel According to Job*
Mason, Mike. *The Mystery of Marriage*
Miller, Paul. *A Praying Life: Connecting with God in a Distracting World*
Montgomery, L.M. *Emily Climbs*
Montgomery, L.M. *The Story Girl*
Mueller, George. *Autobiography of George Mueller*
Murray, Ian. *Jonathan Edwards: A New Biography*
Owen, John. *The Glory of Christ*
Packer, J.I. *Evangelism and the Sovereignty of God*
Piper, John, and Justin Taylor. *A God Entranced Vision of All Things*
Piper, John. *A Hunger for God: Desiring God Through Fasting and Prayer*
Piper, John. *Pierced by the Word*
Piper, John. *The Pleasures of God*
Piper, John. *The Roots of Endurance*
Piper, John. *What Jesus Demands from the World*
Spurgeon, Charles. *Lectures to My Students*
Torrey, R.A. *How to Pray*
Tozer, A. W. *God Tells the Man Who Cares*
Ware, Bruce. *God's Greater Glory*

Whitney, Donald. *Spiritual Disciplines for the Christian Life*
Whyte, Alexander. *Lord Teach Us to Pray*

## For Further Reading on the Subject of Prayer

Bennett, Arthur. *The Valley of Vision: Puritan Prayers and Devotions*
Beeke, Joel. *Taking Hold of God: Reformed and Puritan Perspectives on Prayer*
Calvin, John. *The Institutes of Christian Religion* (Book 3)
Johnstone, Patrick, *Operation World: A day-to-day guide to praying for the world*
Keller, Timothy. *Prayer: Experiencing Awe and Intimacy with God*
Miller, Paul. *A Praying Life: Connecting with God in a Distracting World*
Piper, John. *Desiring God* (Chapter 6)
Piper, John. *When I Don't Desire God: How to Fight for Joy*
Whitney, Donald. *Praying the Bible*

## ABOUT THE AUTHOR

Andrew Case grew up on the mission field in Oaxaca, Mexico, and is a graduate of The Southern Baptist Theological Seminary and the Canada Institute of Linguistics. Currently he serves as a Bible translation consultant in Equatorial Guinea along with his wife Bethany. Besides writing both fiction and nonfiction, his joys include teaching, preaching, dinosaurs, L.M. Montgomery, and song-writing. His music is available through all major online outlets, and is regularly downloaded in over fifteen different countries. To partner with him in Bible Translation, please visit his website HisMagnificence.com, and click on "Bio." You can follow him at:
www.facebook.com/andrewcasebooks.

## ALSO AVAILABLE FROM ANDREW CASE

### On paperback and Kindle

- *Water of the Word: Intercession for Her*
- *Setting Their Hope in GOD:*
  *Biblical Intercession for Your Children*
- *Prayers of an Excellent Wife*
- *Cristina of Aspen Aisle*

### Free for Android and iOS

*Praying the Light*

These books do *not* exist to make money. They exist to edify the Church, spread and deepen a passion for Scripture, and adorn the Gospel. This is why they can be found free online (HisMagnificence.com). It is our joy and delight to give freely what has been freely given to us (Matthew 10:8). We never want to make cost "an obstacle in the way of the gospel of Christ" (I Corinthians 9:12).

Made in the USA
Las Vegas, NV
24 November 2023

81380895R00134